PRAISE FOR THE ECOTEAM PROGRAM

(from which *Water Stewardship* is derived)

"This program is the first step-by-step plan for turning environmental concern into action."
The Chicago Tribune

"A movement . . . of unquestionable zeal is challenging consumption at the grass roots . . . local support groups called EcoTeams are methodically helping members reduce the amount and kind of material that flows in and out of homes."
The New York Times

"The program offers a common-sense approach to environmentalism. One participant says, 'I love our neighborhood and this is an opportunity for us to make it an even nicer place to live together'."
The Boston Globe

"The biggest thing about EcoTeams is that they are helping people change behavior. You could do information campaigns and hope people change, but as a city, this is a better investment."
The Kansas City Star

"EcoTeams help people build community while working toward something they believe in. It takes a village to save the Earth."
Family Circle

"The *EcoTeam* Program is skillfully designed to be attractive to individuals, local governments, and businesses . . . It has demonstrated results . . . it can make a real difference. In our work with communities across America, this is exactly the sort of tool for which they are searching."
Molly Olson, Executive Director, President's Council on Sustainable Development (Clinton Administration)

"The *EcoTeam* approach opens up a new category of policy instruments having to do with voluntary change. The program is more sophisticated than information campaigns, since it gives people the personal support they need to change their ingrained habits of how they use resources."
Paul de Jongh, Deputy Director General for Environmental Protection, The Netherlands, Author, Dutch "Green Plan"

"One of the most enlightening and useful programs that I have had the privilege to encounter . . . It provides a starting point for America's citizens and communities to begin the journey of becoming more sustainable."
Michele Perrault, Past President, The Sierra Club

WATER STEWARDSHIP

Water Stewardship

A 30 Day Program to Protect and Conserve Our Water Resources

David Gershon

ISBN 978-0-9644373-7-1
Copyright © 2008 David Gershon

Published by:
Empowerment Institute
P.O. Box 428
Woodstock, New York 12498
www.empowermentinstitute.net

♻ Printed on Recycled Paper

DEDICATION

To the participants of this program who are leaving a legacy of
water stewardship for future generations.

ACKNOWLEDGEMENTS

Eve Baer for program design and photographs, Dan Wetzel for illustrations, and Steve Busch for graphic design. Elenor Hodges, Tom Kelsch, Annette Mills, John Tippett, and Aileen Winquist for their support in the development of the program.

TABLE OF CONTENTS

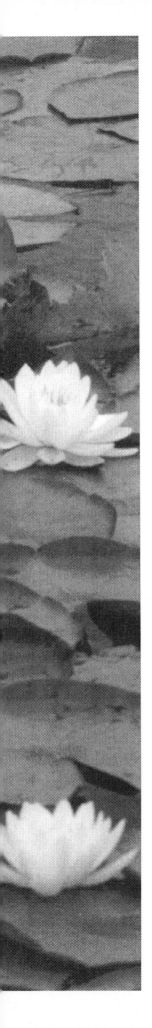

HOW THE PROGRAM WORKS:

1. This program will help you take the necessary actions to better steward your community's precious water resources.

2. You can do the program either with your household family members or as part of a peer support group of friends, neighbors, co-workers, or members of your faith community or civic organization—an EcoTeam. A good size for an EcoTeam is 5 to 8 households.

3. In either format, the program is designed to be completed in 4 meetings that take place every 10 to 14 days. A team initiator runs the meetings using scripts located in the support section of this workbook. Meetings last 1.5 to 2 hours, with several hours needed between meetings to take the actions selected. If you do the program as an individual household and live with others, turn your household members into a team and adapt the meeting scripts accordingly. If you live alone and choose to do this on your own, use the program's suggested time sequence as a structure to keep you motivated.

4. The first meeting is devoted to team-building. This is the foundation for all the work that follows. You will prepare for the program, build a team, and learn about your current environmental impact and opportunities to make improvements.

5. Before each meeting, you read all the actions from the related workbook pages and decide which ones you will take. Then in the Action Log, located at the beginning of each section, enter the day and time you plan to do them. If you live with others, discuss your plan with them to get their ideas and participation. Bring your Action Log to the meeting along with any requests you might have for team support.

6. At the meeting, you review actions taken over the prior two weeks and share your action plan for the next two weeks. Your team will then help you fine-tune your plan and provide support and inspiration to carry it out.

7. That's it! Have fun as you make life better for your family, neighbors, and all those who partake in nature's fragile ecosystem.

ABOUT SELECTING ACTIONS

The water you use to drink, wash, and cook comes from a watershed near your home. A watershed is the land that water flows across or under on its way to a stream or river. Every community, whether it is mountainous or flat, urban

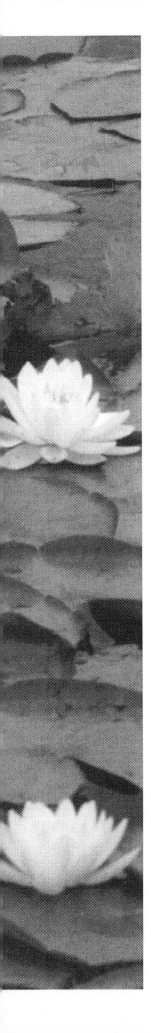

or rural, is part of a watershed. Within each watershed, all water drains to the lowest point, carrying with it soil particles, oil, road salt, organic materials, pesticides, and fertilizers.

This program is designed to help you reduce your impact on your watershed and those into which it feeds. To achieve this, you need to develop water-friendly lifestyle practices that reduce your pollution, storm water volume, and water consumption.

Reducing pollutants: Water running off your lawn, roads, and other surfaces picks up nutrients, bacteria, and chemicals and carries them directly into the streams and rivers. These pollutants can cause a variety of problems for living things—including humans—that live in or interact with your streams and rivers. For example, extra nutrients from fertilizer cause too much algae to grow, which robs the water of oxygen and makes it a bad place for fish, snails, and other stream dwellers to live. If the water isn't a healthy habitat for these critters, this in turn affects animals that are higher in the food chain, like mammals and birds.

Reducing storm water volume: Another major problem for streams and rivers is the sheer volume of stormwater that flows into them. Stormwater from all parts of the watershed is concentrated in the storm drain system and carried to your waterways at very high speeds. When the water finally reaches the streams, it blasts adjacent stream channels, causing them to become wider and deeper. The soil eroded from streambanks during storms smothers aquatic habitat. Over time, this sediment is carried downstream to where it combines with sediment from other urban streams in the watershed. This sediment is one of the main contributors to unhealthy waterways.

Reducing water consumption: Wastewater from your consumption flows back into your streams and rivers, either through the wastewater treatment plant or into your storm drains, untreated. Using less tap water prevents unnecessary chemical treatment and disposal from the treatment plant. And by not overwatering your yard, you can help prevent too much water—and pollutants—from entering our streams and rivers. If a community is facing a drought, then conserving water helps ensure that there is enough for everyone.

As you decide which actions to do, remember this: The actions in the *Water Quality* section will reduce both pollutants and the volume of stormwater coming from your yard. The actions in the *Water Conservation* section will reduce unnecessary water usage.

Section One:
Water Quality Actions

INTRODUCTION

Images of our neighborhood streams, rivers, lakes, and reservoirs include hiking and biking trails; glimpses of resident wildlife; parks; and peaceful natural refuges. For thousands of years, these water bodies have been wildlife-rich, self-sustaining homes to many types of fish and other aquatic life. Today both plant and animal life struggle to survive as they face the increasing pressures of urban development. But there is good news . . . we know the prescription for our water's health, and it starts with us. By developing simple, water-protection lifestyle practices, each of us can make a huge difference.

Equally exciting is the fact that the same practices that help restore our water resources also make our neighborhoods more livable. Imagine a neighborhood where green space is the rule and asphalt is the exception. Imagine a community where every piece of the landscape is utilized as a water-purifying filter. Imagine a residential street where the attractive landscape invites you to stroll down it. Imagine a neighborhood where you'd really like to live.

You can make it happen right where you live. You can transform your neighborhood, starting with your own daily practices and some relatively straightforward landscaping.

WATER QUALITY ACTION LOG

Action	Location	Time	Cost	Action Plan Date/Time	(✓) Discussed with Household
1. TOXIC SLEUTH – Reducing toxic products in your household	Home	⧗⧗	♦		
2. A NATURAL LAWN – Reducing your use of weed killers and fertilizers on your lawn	Yard	⧗⧗	♦♦		
3. A GREEN GARDENER – Reducing your use of toxic garden products in your garden	Yard	⧗⧗	♦♦		
4. CUT IT HIGH AND LET IT LIE – Mulching grass	Yard	⧗	♦		
5. LET IT ROT – Backyard composting	Yard	⧗⧗	♦♦		
6. POOP SCOOP – Cleaning up after your dog	Neighborhood	⧗	♦		
7. DON'T BE AN OIL DRIP – Identifying and fixing oil leaks on your vehicles	Car	⧗	♦ – ♦♦		
8. NO PHOS-FOR-US – Washing your car with the least environmental impact	Car	⧗	♦		
9. DOWN BY THE STREAM – Creating a streamside "Grow Zone"	Neighborhood	⧗⧗⧗	♦♦		
10. A NO RAINER – Installing a rain barrel or downspout extension	Yard	⧗⧗	♦♦♦		
11. CATCH IT WHILE YOU CAN – Creating a rain garden	Yard	⧗⧗⧗	♦♦♦		
12. YARD MAKEOVER – Creating water-friendly landscaping	Yard	⧗⧗⧗	♦♦♦		
13. LET THE GROUND SHOW THROUGH – Reducing paved surfaces	Yard	⧗⧗⧗	♦♦ – ♦♦♦		
14. THE ROAD LESS TRAVELED – Reducing vehicle miles traveled	Car	⧗⧗	♦		
15. LEAK NOT – Remediating oil storage tank leaks	Yard	⧗ – ⧗⧗⧗	♦ – ♦♦♦		

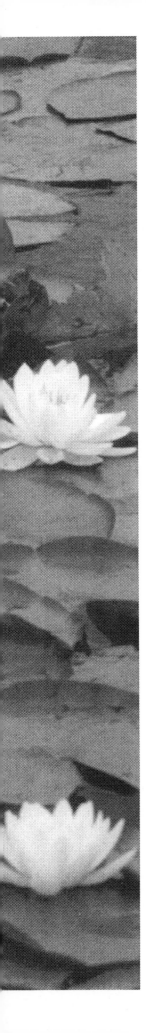

1. TOXIC SLEUTH

Reducing Toxic Products in Your Household

WHY ACT?

Products we use to clean and fix up our homes, care for our yards and cars, and keep the bugs away need to be used with care for our sake and that of our water. Toxic products that are spread on the ground or washed down the drain can harm the soil, pollute local waterways, and affect the biological organisms used to treat our wastewater. This water action will help you identify harmful products and substitute them with water-friendly alternatives.

WATER ACTION

- ○ Make a list of products in your home that might be toxic.
    - Search all the places in your home where these products may be found: under sinks, in the kitchen closet, laundry room, workroom, shed, or garage.
    - If the words "danger," "warning," and/or "caution" appear on the label, it may be hazardous to you and our environment. If you have any questions, call your local household hazardous waste program (see Resources). You might also call the 800 number on the label, if there is one, and ask the company about its product.
- ○ Find water-friendly products that will achieve the same results.
    - Call your local health food store, supermarket, or hardware store to see whether they have environmentally friendly products that you could use to replace the toxic ones.
    - If your local stores do not routinely stock environmentally friendly products, ask them to carry these items.
- ○ Use up what you have or call your local hazardous waste program to find out where to properly dispose of the toxic products.
- ○ If you must use toxic products, be sure to store them safely where children and animals can't get to them.

MATERIALS

Paper and pen, phone, environmentally friendly household products

TIME

Two to three hours

RESOURCES

If you wish to make your own environmentally friendly cleaners go to http://www.greenhome.com/info/articles/Household_Cleaners/74/

BENEFITS

By making your home a water-friendly zone, you've protected your immediate quality of life. You are also protecting the quality of life for all of us!

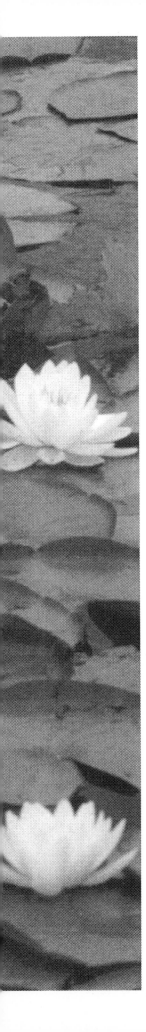

2. A Natural Lawn
Reducing Your Use of Weed Killers and Fertilizers on Your Lawn

WHY ACT?

If you have a lawn, you may be using weed killers and fertilizers to keep it green and weed-free. Unfortunately, toxic chemicals in weed killers and fertilizers often wash off your lawn into local streams and ground water, eventually polluting our waterways and their tributaries. Fertilizer encourages algae growth, and when the algae die and decompose, the oxygen in the water is reduced. Pesticides, even in very small amounts, can harm or kill aquatic life. Exposure to chemicals has also been linked to human health problems. This water action will show you how to create a natural lawn and help protect the health of your family, wildlife, and our local resources.

WATER ACTION

- ○ Get your soil tested and apply fertilizers only at the appropriate time in the right amounts.
- ○ If you fertilize at all, use organic compost instead of chemical fertilizers. Fertilizers act as pollutants once they enter our waterways. You can either create your own compost, or purchase it from a garden supply center.
- ○ Accept a few weeds, like clover, which can coexist nicely with your lawn. Hand pull the ugly ones before they seed, and leave the others alone.
- ○ Overseed thin areas in the spring and fall to crowd out weeds. Just rake to expose the soil, spread the seed, and cover with 1/4 inch of compost or soil.

Note: To lessen the burden of maintaining a lawn and the toll it takes on the water supply and the pollutants going into the watershed, consider replacing all or part of your lawn with native trees, shrubs, ferns, wildflowers, and groundcover (see *Yard Makeover,* Action 12, pg. 25).

MATERIALS

Natural compost, soil, seeds, rake, and weed pulling tools

TIME

A couple of hours to pull weeds and fertilize with compost

BENEFITS

By "greening" your lawn, you prevent the pollution from weed killers and fertilizers from flowing into streams and rivers while making your lawn a natural place for you, your family and neighbors to enjoy.

3. A Green Gardener

Reducing Your Use of Toxic Pesticides, Herbicides, and Fertilizers in Your Garden

WHY ACT?

Whether you are growing gorgeous flowers or delicious tomatoes, consider doing this without using toxic pesticides, herbicides, and fertilizers. These chemicals can harm children, pets, and local wildlife and kill helpful insects such as ladybugs and green lacewings that keep real pests in check. Even when used sparingly, these chemicals can end up washing down storm drains into streams and eventually polluting the local water supply. This water action will help you be a truly green gardener.

WATER ACTION

❍ To naturally strengthen the resistance of your plants to pests, build healthy soil. Use compost. Make your own compost or purchase it (see *Let It Rot, Action 5,* pg. 14).

❍ Choose native plants that are naturally pest-resistant and adapted to our climate.

❍ If unwelcome pests do appear, pull them off by hand or spray them with a diluted solution of phosphate-free soapy water. You can also pick off the affected part of the plant. Remember that insects are part of your garden's ecosystem. The occasional pest in your garden may also be a food source for beneficial insects, amphibians, and birds. Learn to live with the occasional pest.

Note: If you must use fertilizers or pesticides, read the labels and follow all safety precautions. Use sparingly on a dry, windless day. Take leftover chemicals to a household hazardous waste collection site.

MATERIALS

Compost, organic fertilizer, soap and water; pesticides as a last resort

TIME

A few hours to prepare your garden and some time to take care of it

BENEFITS

By "greening" your garden, you prevent fertilizers, toxic pesticides, and herbicides from flowing into the water systems, all while making your garden a natural place for you, your family, and neighbors to enjoy. You protect your family's health, and the health of your neighbors. You also save the lives of local and beneficial wildlife.

4. Cut It High and Let It Lie
Mulching Grass

WHY ACT?

Your grass clippings can account for as much as 50% of your yard waste during the peak growing seasons. You can leave these clippings on the lawn to feed the soil. This practice is known as "grasscycling." It enhances the health of your lawn by adding moisture and acting as a natural fertilizer. It also saves you time—no more bagging clippings and dragging them to the curb! This water action will walk you through the grasscycling steps.

WATER ACTION

❍ Mow your lawn to between 2 and 2½ inches to hide clippings.
❍ Leave the clippings on the lawn. They will break down quickly and not result in thatch.
❍ Mow the lawn when it's dry to avoid clumping.
❍ Water deeply, but infrequently. (If you have clay soil, it is better to water more frequently for a shorter period of time.)
❍ If you need a new mower, consider a push mower or an electric mulching lawn mower. The best mulching mowers can blow finely chopped clippings down into your lawn where they disappear from sight, decompose, and fertilize the lawn quickly. An electric mulching mower also cuts down on air pollution, and a push mower eliminates it completely!

Note: To lessen the burden of maintaining a lawn and the toll it takes on our water supply, consider replacing all or part of your lawn with drought-tolerant plants, herbs, and wildflowers.

MATERIALS

Lawnmower and a yard!

TIME

Grasscycling will substantially reduce the time you are spending on lawn care. Specifics will depend on the size of your lawn.

BENEFITS

By grasscycling, you save valuable water resources and provide natural fertilizer for your lawn.

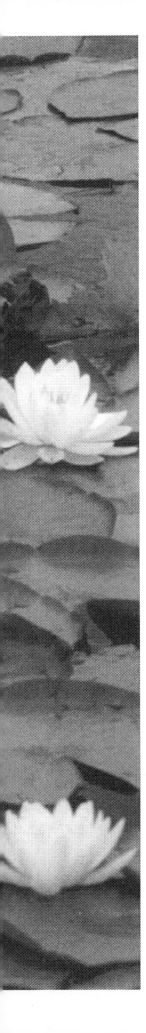

5. LET IT ROT
Backyard Composting

WHY ACT?

Garden trimmings, leaves, and grass clippings are "waste" only if you treat them that way! Up to a third of the material you set at the curb for disposal is yard waste that could be composted and turned into yard treasure. Composting, a process that turns your yard waste into choice fertilizer, can be used to enrich the soil in your yard and garden. A compost pile can be as simple and cost-free as the recipe below or as state-of-the-art as a store-bought compost bin. By keeping yard waste in your yard rather than at the curb, you can keep it from washing into storm drains. This water action will show you how to assist Nature in her magic.

WATER ACTION

○ Create a compost pile, build your own compost bin, or purchase one from a store or catalog.
○ Although there are a lot of ways to compost, here's one tried-and-true method:
  - Place your pile or bin in an area of your yard that is both shady and sure to receive rain.
  - Chop or shred yard waste before putting it in the pile or bin. For best results, use a combination of green and brown materials (e.g., grass clippings and leaves).
  - Mix materials with a pitchfork, adding water as needed. A handful of compost should feel like a wrung-out sponge.
  - Mix the pile every 2-3 weeks. If the middle is dry, turn and moisten the materials. If the pile is woody and not decomposing, mix in fresh grass clippings or other green plant trimmings.
○ In six months or so, the bottom and center of the pile should be ready to use; as mulch around your yard, as an amendment to garden soil, or combined with sand as a potting mix.
○ To take composting one step further, consider recycling your food waste by setting up a "vermicompost." Vermicomposting is a way of recycling food waste using red worms (i.e., fishing worms) in an enclosed bin. Another alternative is to use a commercially distributed compost container that is enclosed and off the ground.

MATERIALS

Yard waste, pitchfork, compost bin (plus red worms and/or an enclosed bin if you want to recycle your food waste).

TIME

About 1-2 hours for set-up and a few minutes every couple of weeks for care

RESOURCES

There are many companies that sell compost bins in various shapes and sizes, at a wide range of prices. Search under "compost bin" on the Internet. If you want to try vermicomposting, go to www.wormwoman.com.

BENEFITS

Composting helps keep grass, leaves, and other yard material from washing into storm drains. The finished "treasure" eliminates the need for chemical fertilizer and, when used as mulch, conserves water—further reducing the negative impact on streams and rivers. By being a player in Nature's wonder, you also help save taxpayer dollars by avoiding collection and disposal costs for yard waste set at the curb!

6. POOP SCOOP
Cleaning Up After Your Dog

WHY ACT?

Poop pollutes. Our pet's waste is a health risk when deposited on streets and lawns. It can be washed down storm drains and end up in the stream. The bacteria, together with other pollutants, can make the water unsafe for swimming and cause health hazards for humans and aquatic life.. This water action will show you how to take care of your pet's poop without polluting your neighborhood and its water quality.

WATER ACTION

- ○ When walking your pet, bring a small trowel or "pooper-scooper" and a plastic bag.
- ○ Make sure your pet does not pee directly on the pavement. It is less likely the next rainstorm will wash the waste into the storm drains or local tributaries. Also avoid planted areas and your neighbor's yard. Choose a grassy area instead where you can easily pick up your pet's poop, and where your pet's pee will not bother anyone or harm plants.
- ○ After your pet does its business, scoop the poop and place it in the bag. Tie it shut until you get home.
- ○ Flush the poop down the toilet so it can be treated in the community sewage or septic system. Your other alternatives are to bury the poop six inches deep in the ground or place the bag in your garbage can.

MATERIALS

Trowel or "pooper-scooper," plastic bag or container

TIME

A minute or two to scoop and flush

BENEFITS

You help keep the watershed healthy, protecting fish and wildlife habitats. You also improve the neighborhood for all to enjoy, while giving children a cleaner, healthier place to play.

7. Don't Be an Oil Drip
Identifying and Fixing Oil Leaks on Your Vehicles

WHY ACT?

Oil and other fluids that leak from your car are washed from the street into tributaries and storm drains that flow directly into our streams and rivers. In the U.S., it is estimated that petroleum washed off the pavement every year, along with oil dumped into storm drains, sends 15 times more oil into the ocean than the Exxon Valdez did. This water action will help you reduce harmful oil runoff from your vehicle.

WATER ACTION

This water action has two parts: check for oil leaks, and fix them.

- ❍ Before you drive away, simply back up one car length and check the ground for any oil leaks where you were parked.
- ❍ If you find an oil leak, call your local repair shop to fix it, or make a plan to repair it as soon as possible. Consider using recycled oil.
  - Clean up spills immediately. You can purchase a non-toxic biodegradable chemical that will safely break down oil deposits from your local hardware or boat marine store. If you can't find this item, consider using kitty litter to soak up oil. Place it in your garbage can in a sealed bag.
  - When parked in your driveway, keep a drip pan under the leak until you repair it. Empty the collected fluids into a tightly sealed and labeled container, and recycle it.
- ❍ Until your oil leak is repaired, use alternative transportation: carpool, bus, bicycle, or walk.

Note: Boat owners should look around the waterline for leaks or spills before leaving the dock. Always check for oil leaks inside the bilge before draining. If you discover a leak, call your local repair shop to fix it or make a plan to repair it as soon as possible.

MATERIALS

Phone number of local mechanic, drip pan, biodegradable material to break down the oil leak, plastic sealable container

TIME

A minute to check for leaks; more time for repairs

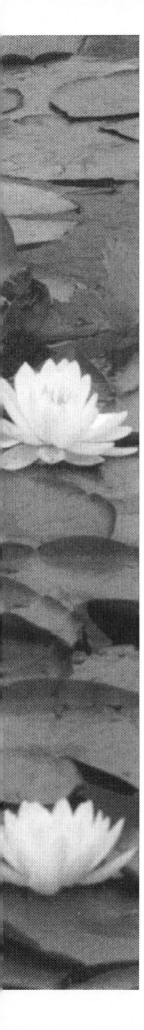

BENEFITS

You prevent hazardous oil from draining into local water sources, thus protecting natural habitats, wildlife, and water from contamination. One pint of motor oil can contaminate 125,000 gallons of drinking water and make an oil slick about the size of two football fields. Your efforts have a huge impact.

8. NO PHOS-FOR-US

Washing Your Car with the Least Environmental Impact

WHY ACT?

How and where you wash your car or truck makes a difference to our local environment! The soap, together with dirt and oil washed from your vehicle, can find its way into local streams, wells, and groundwater through storm drains, which are not linked to a water treatment plant. Runoff of excess phosphorous contributes to the decline in health of streams and rivers. This pollution harms water quality and aquatic life. This water action will help you keep your vehicle and your waters clean.

WATER ACTION

- ○ To have the least environmental impact, go to a car wash that treats and recycles the wash water. Most car washes do this; check with them to confirm. If you take your car to be washed at a charity event, make sure they have a storm drain catchment kit to trap oil and other harmful chemicals.
- ○ If you're a "do-it-yourselfer," wash your vehicle on grass or gravel instead of the street or driveway to help filter the soapy water and grime. If you drive your car onto the grass, take care to avoid driving near any trees so you do not damage the tree roots.
- ○ Use soap that is biodegradable. To conserve water, make sure your hose has an on-off switch or nozzle.
- ○ If you use a bucket of soap and water, pour what is left in your bucket down the sink so it can be treated.

MATERIALS

Hose, nozzle, bucket, sponges or rags, biodegradable soap, a lawn or a gravel area to park, commercial car wash

TIME

No extra time required

BENEFITS

Your efforts protect aquatic habitats and water quality.

9. Down by the Stream
Creating a Streamside "Grow Zone"

WHY ACT?

If a stream or drainage ditch runs through your property, the health of your streamside ecosystem is in jeopardy if you have invasive, non-native plants or monoculture vegetation, both of which contribute to soil erosion. To create a sustainable streamside ecosystem you need to have diverse, native, and multi-storied vegetation. Native plants need little or no watering. By "going native," you'll also reduce the need for pollutants such as fertilizers, pesticides, and herbicides. This water action will help you protect your property and will support and protect fish and wildlife habitat. You and other residents will enjoy the benefits of clean water and its recreational opportunities.

WATER ACTION

○ Don't mow down to your stream. Leave at least 5 feet in native plant buffer.
○ If you have invasive, non-native vegetation or monoculture vegetation (a single type of plant), re-vegetate with native, ecologically diverse plants of varying heights.
○ If your stream bank has begun to erode, seek expert help to repair it.

MATERIALS

Garden tools and gloves, native plants, phone, and directory for nurseries and expertise

TIME

A few hours to several days, depending on the extent of the problem

BENEFITS

You will contribute to fish spawning habitat by reducing the clouding of streams caused by erosion. Hardy, streamside, native vegetation also helps filter out pollutants that may have otherwise entered the stream. You will also contribute to the preservation of your own property by stemming streamside erosion.

10. A No Rainer

Installing a Rain Barrel or Downspout Extension

WHY ACT?

Water running off your roof during a rainstorm can be part of the problem—or a resource you can put to good use! On many properties, rooftop rainwater drains onto yards with compacted clay soil or onto hard pavement. In either case, it eventually flows into storm drains and directly into our local streams. Reducing storm water runoff is the first step to reviving life in urban streams. This water action will show you how to divert and store rainwater runoff, so that you can help support aquatic life and reduce stream bank erosion. What's more, rainwater collection can help you save water for use in your yard, eliminate potential flooding in your basement, and reduce storm water management costs.

WATER ACTION

○ Check your gutters and roof drains and remove any leaves or other debris that may block water flow. If leaf accumulation is a recurring problem, consider installing commercial gutter shields.

○ If your roof drain downspouts discharge too close to the house, install extensions that carry the water at least six feet away from the foundation to a vegetated area of your yard. Use additional pieces of downspout or open gutters for the extensions. Place a splash block at the end of the extension to spread out the water as it runs onto your lawn. This reduces the potential for soil erosion.

○ Consider installing a rain barrel at the end of your downspout to collect rainwater (see Resources for purchase and installation information).

○ You can use the rainwater to water plants and shrubs between rainfalls or allow the water to dribble out slowly so your yard can soak it up and recharge the groundwater.

MATERIALS

Ladder, gloves, and eye protection to wear while cleaning gutters; cistern or rain barrel, connectors, hose for outflow

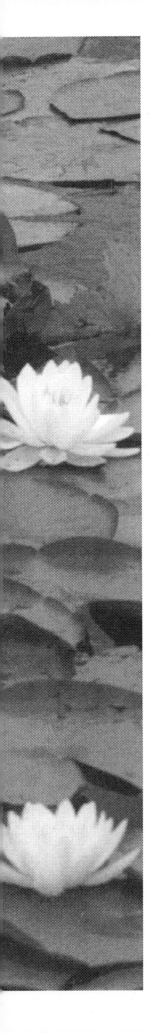

TIME

One to six hours, depending on gutter maintenance and size of cistern

RESOURCES

American Rainwater Catchment Systems Association: www.arcsa-usa.org
Urban Garden Center: www.urbangardencenter.com
Rainsaver USA: www.rainsaverusa.com

BENEFITS

You reduce the volume of stormwater entering our streams, while creating a source of water for your yard between rainfalls. In addition, since rooftop runoff is a major cause of wet or flooded basements, cisterns and rain barrels are often the most cost-effective way to keep water from entering your basement.

11. CATCH IT WHILE YOU CAN
Creating a Rain Garden

WHY ACT?

A rain garden is an attractive native plant garden with a special purpose: to reduce the amount of stormwater that rushes into our streams and other waterways. It is constructed as a place to direct the stormwater that falls on your property and is landscaped with water-loving native plant species. By creating a rain garden in your yard, you can use rain the way nature intended—instead of wasting this valuable resource!

WATER ACTION

- ○ Look for low-lying areas of your yard where water tends to run or collect during a rainstorm.
- ○ Dig out the soil 2-4 feet down, taking care not to destroy any significant roots of nearby trees.
- ○ Mix shredded leaf mulch (available from your municipality) with the soil that you have removed. Refill the hole.
- ○ Place a berm (small mound) along the lower edge of the area you've selected, so you can capture and retain stormwater.
- ○ Plant the garden with water-loving native plants that can handle alternately very wet and dry conditions. Some good choices for shrubs are sweetspire, summer sweet, arrowood viburnum, chokeberry, and winterberry.

MATERIALS

Shovel, processed leaf mulch, native plants

TIME

A few hours or more, depending on the size of the garden

BENEFITS

Your rain garden will help keep water in the ground—where it belongs! It will also add an attractive and interesting new element to your landscape.

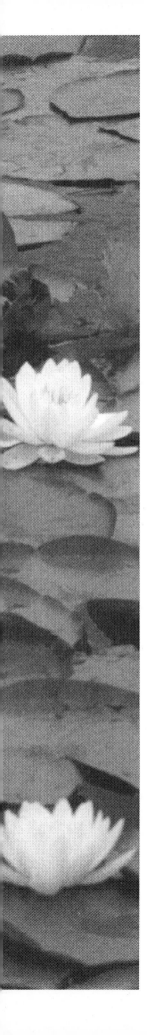

12. YARD MAKEOVER
Creating Water-friendly Landscaping

WHY ACT?

Before your home or subdivision was built, the forest and soil that existed there functioned as a giant sponge and filter. Rainfall was absorbed into the forest soil, and the rich organic layer filtered out any impurities in the water. A typical rainfall didn't result in runoff. The water just filtered into the soil and recharged groundwater.

A conventional housing development site, however, is covered with impervious surfaces that short-circuit Mother Nature's water filtering and recycling plan. The result is that a lot more water runs off into the streams. This increased volume of water erodes stream banks and sends sediment downstream. Moreover, that water tends to be full of pollutants ranging from excess fertilizers to motor oil and even heavy metals from car brake pads. The good news is that you can give your yard a "makeover" that will put the landscape back to work as a filter. A water-saving landscape can be beautiful and highly distinctive. It also provides habitat to local wildlife. Best of all, your yard makeover makes your community more livable by creating attractive green space!

WATER ACTION

❍ Develop a plan for creating a more natural landscape. It's done by planting native trees and other native plants that can survive well on the normal rainfall of our region. Your goal is to reduce the percentage of lawn in your yard.

❍ In creating your plan, seek advice about native plants from your municipal arborist, extension service agent, or the National Wildlife Federation, www.nwf.org. To provide a more diverse, natural topography, consider creating gradual depressions in the landscape that will allow small amounts of rainwater to sink into the ground (see *Catch It While You Can,* Action 11, pg. 24).

❍ To make the transition from lawn to a more water absorbent natural landscape, try this method, which works best if you start in the fall:
- In the parts of your yard you wish to makeover, insert a shovel into the ground in a grid pattern every foot, pushing down and wiggling the shovel to loosen the earth. That soil will now be a sponge to absorb runoff and allow it to enter the ground.

- Place a single layer of newspaper over the lawn, and cover it with two inches of shredded leaf mulch (available from your municipal government).
- Determine where you walk in your yard, and lay down thick wood mulch for your paths.
- After a few months of leaf mulch decomposition, plant native trees, shrubs, ferns, wildflowers, and groundcover.

MATERIALS

Newspaper, shredded leaf mulch, wood mulch, native plants, gardening tools

TIME

Several hours to plan and considerable time and pleasure to create your new landscape (minus all the time you will save by not having to mow or maintain your lawn!)

BENEFITS

You'll keep a lot of rainwater from running down your street and into storm drains and streams. Further, you'll reduce up to 50% of your yearly water use, save the time and money spent keeping up a green lawn, and attract birds and butterflies to your new backyard habitat!

13. LET THE GROUND SHOW THROUGH
Reducing Paved Surfaces

WHY ACT?

This is one of the most important water actions you can take toward helping to improve our local streams and rivers. Did you ever consider how much water runs off your property during a rainstorm? Every time there's a heavy rain, hundreds—even thousands—of gallons of water fall on your roof, driveway, patio, and other paved surfaces. These surfaces are called "impervious" because it is impossible for the water to penetrate them. Instead of seeping back into the ground, the water rushes from your property into storm drains, picking up chemicals, litter, oil, and other pollutants along the way. From the storm drains it flows directly into local streams, untreated. The large volume of water that flows into our streams during a rainstorm flushes life out of our waterways, erodes stream banks, and leaves excessively low levels of water in the stream after a rain.

WATER ACTION

○ Analyze how much of your property is covered with paved surface. Make a list of all the impervious surface, including your roof, driveway, patio, and other paved areas.

○ When it comes time to repave your driveway, front walk, or other pathways, choose gravel, wood mulch, or open-design pavers such as flat stones, bricks, or pre-cast concrete lattice pavers. Place the new cover on well-drained soil or on a sand or gravel bed, so that rainwater can soak into the ground. (If weeds grow in the spaces between pavers, consider introducing moss as a natural way to crowd out weeds and make the area more attractive.)

○ If you want to take action right away, decide where you could most easily remove impervious surface and replace it with wood mulch, gravel, soil, or alternative pavers.
  - Start with one small area or project, and expand from there.
  - Remove the paved surface or compacted soil using a pick or hire a contractor to remove the pavement for you.
  - Break up the compacted soil underneath, and add shredded leaf mulch to help the soil retain water.
  - Cover with the pervious surface of your choice, as indicated above.

○ If you're thinking about building an addition on your house, consider building up—not out.

Note: If your goal is 100% permeable surface on your property, you will want to begin looking into "green roof" technology, in which the roof is covered with sod and other vegetation.

MATERIALS

Pick and shovel or a phone book (if you're hiring a contractor), shredded leaf mulch, wood mulch, gravel, soil, or other pervious cover

TIME

An hour or two to plan, and several more to implement your plan

RESOURCES

If you're interested in exploring green roof technology, visit www.greenroofs.com.

BENEFITS

By replacing hard surface with porous surface, you will allow water to be absorbed into the ground. Not only will you save thousands of gallons of rainwater from running into the storm drains and into the stream—you are helping to replenish our groundwater at a time when water is more precious than ever!

14. THE ROAD LESS TRAVELED

Reducing Vehicle Miles Traveled

WHY ACT?

Experts estimate that approximately one-third of our water pollution comes from particulate matter that started out as air pollution. Automobiles are our primary local source of air pollution. The amount of vehicle miles traveled (VMT) per household is increasing dramatically every year which in turn is causing a significant environmental impact. And the more miles we drive our cars, the more we contribute to global warming and the depletion of our non-renewable energy resources. Many describe unconstrained automobile use as the greatest environmental problem facing our cities and towns today. Perhaps the most significant single step you can take toward sustainable living is to reduce the amount of single occupancy vehicle miles you travel each year. This action will support you in this endeavor.

WATER ACTION

❍ Start by inviting each household member who drives a car to join you in the learning experience. Have each driver keep an automobile trip diary for two typical weeks. Note the destination and mileage of each trip. Divide the trips into categories including: combinable, recreational, and other modes available (bus, bike, walking, car/van pool).

❍ At the end of two weeks, add up the miles traveled by you and the other members of your household in each category. Project this over a year, including any trips you normally take that didn't fall into this two-week period.

❍ Now the fun begins. Create a plan to reduce your household's single occupancy vehicle miles traveled by between 20% and 50% over the next year. With forethought and careful planning, these goals are achievable for most people. What's needed is creativity. You might be motivated by increasing the amount of time in your life, saving money, or seeing this as creating a personal environmental legacy to future generations. As part of your plan, write your motivation and the benefits you hope to achieve from taking this action.

❍ Following are some examples of how you might choose your VMT reduction target.

- Work: Telecommuting, carpooling, riding public transportation, walking or biking one day each week will reduce your commute VMT by 20%, two days a week by 40%.

- Food shopping and household errands: Going twice as long between routine errands by making a list and buying in larger quantities could

reduce VMT in this category by as much as 50% a week.
- Children's school and after school activities: Carpooling with other parents could reduce this category of VMT by 20% to 80%.

○ If you evaluate each typical trip this way, you will be amazed at what is possible with relatively little effort and forethought! Most of us are just habituated to our autos as our primary means of mobility. With a little creativity and effort to make the initial change, we will soon get just as habituated to a more environmentally sustainable means of transportation.

MATERIALS

Your automobile, pen, paper, creativity, bike, walking shoes, bus pass, etc.

TIME

A minute or so each car trip for two weeks to record your mileage; an hour or two to create your VMT reduction plan; significantly more free time for other things through your increased transportation efficiency

RESOURCES

Car Alternatives: www.commuterpage.com/carfreealt.htm

BENEFITS

You will reduce the amount of polluted exhaust, motor oil, brake and transmission fluid, rubber particles, heavy metals, and other toxic substances that will enter our waterways. You will also reduce your use of non-renewable fossil fuels while extending the life expectancy of your car and the roads, improving air quality, and reducing your contribution to global warming. Also, for every mile less traveled, you have more money and time to spend on other things.

15. LEAK NOT
Remediating Oil Storage Tank Leaks

WHY ACT?

Over the last several years, the number of reported leaking heating oil tanks has increased noticeably. Because of the fragility of our waterways, any leaking oil tanks in our watershed area can cause major environmental deterioration to the health of our beautiful rivers and streams.

Finding, fixing and removing old and leaking oil tanks is one of the most important actions that you can take to maintain the health of our waterways. This water action will help you identify a leak if you have one, and provide directions if removal is necessary.

WATER ACTION

○ Do the following home audit to ensure that your oil tank is in good working condition and not leaking.

- Is there water in the tank (record measurement, if taken).
- Is vent line clear?
- Is fill gauge (if one is installed) functioning?
- Is overfill whistle (if one is installed) functioning?
- If tank is aboveground, check the entire tank surface (rust, dents, etc.) for damage.
- If tank is aboveground, check tank support (is it sturdy/solid?).
- Check all pipeline connections (if visible).
- Check oil/water separator (if present), newer models are metal, older are glass (which can shatter during freezing temperatures), drain if needed. If you are unsure, talk to your heating professional.
- Check the fill cap (if damaged/missing, replace immediately—oil can overflow if too much water enters tank.)
- Are there any problems with the operation of the furnace?
- Are there any signs of unexplained dead or withered vegetation in the area?
- Are there any signs of spills or overfills around the fill pipe or vent lines?
- Are there any petroleum vapors in basement/crawl space?
- Check sump pump or floor drain (if present) for petroleum odors or signs of petroleum.
- Look for any signs of oil (odors, sheen on water surfaces, visible puddles of oil, etc.) on property.

○ If you determine your oil tank is in need of repair or you encounter any sudden changes in fuel level, call your heating repair professional or oil supplier for assistance.

Note: Tank closure work should be conducted by a professional. Check local codes and ordinances.

MATERIALS
Phone book, pen, and paper

TIME
This Action can take minutes to check for leaks and hours to fix them. Time well spent.

BENEFITS
Beautiful, oil-free waterways!

NOTES

_____

_____

_____

_____

_____

_____

_____

_____

_____

_____

SECTION TWO:
WATER CONSERVATION ACTIONS

INTRODUCTION

Water is the substance of life on this planet; 80% of the Earth's surface is water, and less than 1% is available and potable. It is 70% of our body weight. It is the principle substance that runs through our veins. It is one of the primary things we bequeath to our children to enable them to live. To be stewards of this precious resource requires that we use it carefully. Unfortunately, we are not doing this. Our wasteful practices and the pollution of our groundwater are deteriorating the available supplies.

Even in places where the water supply still seems adequate, extensive water use causes environmental problems. Great amounts of energy are used to transport, heat, and treat water, using up our fossil fuels and contributing to air pollution and global warming. Water from underground aquifers is often being used faster than it is replenished. Not only will the aquifers run out at some point, but cave-ins in the emptying aquifers damage them in ways that cannot be repaired.

At a personal level, reducing water use will lower your water and sewer bills, or if you have a well, it will lower your utility bills, since electricity is required to pump and heat the water. Stewarding our precious and finite supply of water is an essential part of living an environmentally sustainable lifestyle. In this section, you will learn how to implement the lifestyle practices needed to be a responsible steward of the elixir of life.

WATER CONSERVATION ACTION LOG

KEY:

Average Time:
⧖ = 1 hour or less
⧖⧖ = 1–5 hours
⧖⧖⧖ = 5 hours or more

Typical Cost$
♦ = low or no cost
♦♦ = $10–$100
♦♦♦ = $100 plus

Action	Location	Time	Cost	Action Plan Date/Time	(✓) Discussed with Household
16. AQUA COP – Finding and fixing water leaks in your home	Home	⧖	♦		
17. AQUA TECH – Installing water saving devices	Home	⧖	♦♦		
18. SCRUB-A-DUB-RUB – Reducing water used in personal care	Home	⧖	♦		
19. SCRUB-A-DUB-TUB – Reducing water used to wash dishes	Home	⧖	♦		
20. ALL BOTTLED UP – Drinking refrigerated water	Home	⧖	♦		
21. TANKS A LOT – Reducing water used for toilet flushing	Home	⧖	♦		
22. AM I CLEAN YET? – Reducing water used for showers and baths	Home	⧖	♦		
23. GO WITH THE FLOW – Reducing the number of toilet flushes	Home	⧖	♦		
24. THE LAWN RANGER – Reducing water used for lawns	Yard	⧖	♦♦		
25. A MASTER WATERER – Reducing water used for gardening	Yard	⧖⧖	♦		

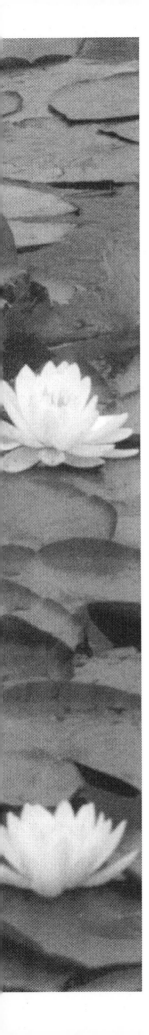

16. Aqua Cop

Finding and Fixing Water Leaks in Your Home

WHY ACT?

A small drip from a leaky faucet isn't a drop in the bucket. A slow leak can waste over 10 gallons of water a day. Add up the water loss from every possible leak in your plumbing and that's a huge amount of wasted water. An EPA study found that a single family home leaks 9.5 gallons per person per day (on average). This water action will help you plug your leaks. It will be time well spent.

WATER ACTION

○ Scout out leaks under sinks and around showers, tubs, and toilets, and make a list. Look for puddles, drips, water stains, and mildew. Listen for toilet tanks that continue to run. Toilet leaks can be silent. To sleuth out a toilet leak, add food coloring to the tank (not the bowl). Don't flush. Instead, check in half an hour to see if any of the dye seeped into the toilet bowl. If it did, you have a leak.

○ If you have a water meter, check to see if it moves while water is not being used. If it does, there is a leak.

○ Call a plumber to fix any leaks, or develop a schedule for repairing them yourself.

Note: Remember to recheck on a regular basis.

MATERIALS

Paper and pencil, food coloring, name and number of plumber, materials to fix leaks you want to repair

TIME

About 15 minutes to check for leaks and call a plumber; more if you fix the leaks yourself

BENEFITS

The more leaks you find, the more water you save. In one day, a steady drip from a faucet can waste 40 gallons of water and a leaking toilet can waste as much as 200 gallons. Your detective skills and caring are helping preserve your community's water supply.

17. Aqua Tech
Installing Water Saving Devices

WHY ACT?

Did you know that showers and faucets account for approximately 30% of your indoor water use? Installing water-saving devices on showers and faucets is an easy and inexpensive way to substantially reduce your water use. Some of these devices have an on-off switch that allows additional savings. And, since showers are more than 50% hot water, you will save on energy as well. If you have older shower and faucet fixtures that are not water efficient, you can benefit from this action.

WATER ACTION

- ○ Call your local hardware store to find out if it stocks low-flow showerheads and faucet aerators for sinks. Purchase them or ask the clerk to special-order the items for you.
- ○ Replace your showerheads and attach the aerators to your faucets.

MATERIALS

Phone book and phone, low-flow showerheads and faucet aerators, preferably with on–off controls

TIME

30 minutes to purchase the items and a few minutes to install them; no extra time to use them

BENEFITS

You can save up to 60% of the water you use while showering and about 50% of the water you use at the sink. If you use the showerhead's on-off control, you will save even more.

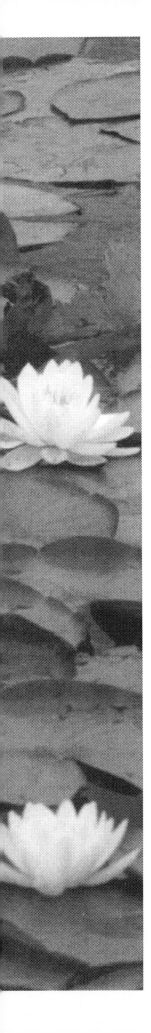

18. SCRUB-A-DUB RUB
Reducing Water Used in Personal Care

WHY ACT?

Does the water run while you wash your face, brush your teeth, or shave? Letting the faucet run just while you brush your teeth—for three minutes in the morning and three minutes at night—uses up to nine gallons of water per day. Shaving with the tap on can easily use another eight gallons. This simple water action will help you reduce your personal water use at the sink by as much as 70%.

WATER ACTION

- To wash hands and face: Run the water at low force to wet your skin and the soap, then turn it off. Wash. Turn the water back on to rinse off.
- To brush your teeth: Run the water at low force to wet your toothbrush, and fill a glass with a little water for rinsing; turn the faucet off. Brush your teeth and rinse. Turn the water on briefly to rinse your brush and glass.
- To shave: Run the water at low force to wet your face and clean and rinse the razor while shaving. Turn off the water when not needed.

MATERIALS

A glass for rinsing

TIME

No additional time

BENEFITS

Making this action a habit saves about 7 gallons of water each day. That's over 2,500 gallons of water every year or the amount of water needed for a five-minute shower every day for over three months! Your awareness goes a long way!

19. SCRUB-A-DUB TUB
Reducing Water Used to Wash Dishes

WHY ACT?

Washing dishes by hand while the water is running for just 10 minutes uses about 15 gallons of water, much of it wasted. This method wastes water even if you turn off the tap while you scrub. Washing a small load in a dishwasher uses up to 12 gallons of water. There is a water-efficient way to wash your dishes, however. This water action will help to reduce the water you use and impress all with your dishwashing skill.

WATER ACTION

❍ Wash dishes in a tub or partitioned sink. Here's how:
  - Fill the tub or section of the sink with hot, soapy water. Use biodegradable liquid soap. Put dishes in and let them soak well.
  - Scrub dishes.
  - Fill a second tub, or the other half of the sink, about two-thirds full with hot water.
  - Dunk and swish dishes in the rinse water to remove soapy film.
❍ Only run the dishwasher when you have a full load.

MATERIALS

Two tubs or a partitioned sink, biodegradable dishwashing liquid

TIME

About 5–10 minutes per meal to wash dishes

BENEFITS

Each time you wash your dishes by hand efficiently, you use about eight gallons of water instead of up to 12. You could save four gallons each day, or almost 1,500 gallons in one year—enough water for six months worth of dishwashing.

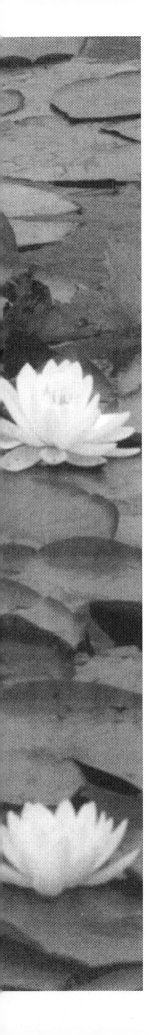

20. All Bottled Up
Drinking Refrigerated Water

WHY ACT?

How much water goes down the drain before you get water cold enough to drink? One cup? Two cups? Six? On average, 24 cups of clean water are wasted each time we wait for the water to turn cold by letting it run for one minute. In cities, this unused water will increase flow to the wastewater treatment plant where it will be chemically treated before being released into streams and rivers. That's not only wasted water but wasted energy to treat the water. This water action will help you reduce to zero the amount of water you let slip down the drain just to get a cold drink!

WATER ACTION

○ Fill a reusable bottle or container with tap water and keep it in the refrigerator. Now you have cold, refreshing drinking water on hand at all times.

MATERIALS

Reusable bottle or container

TIME

About 1 minute to fill the container

BENEFITS

If you've been letting the water run like this once a day, you'll now save about 550 gallons of water per person in your home each year. That's enough water for about 14 baths!

21. TANKS A LOT
Reducing Water Used for Toilet Flushing

WHY ACT?

The tank on the back of many toilets holds about 3.5 gallons of water. Only 1.6 gallons are needed per flush, but all 3.5 go down the drain. This easy water action will help you reduce the amount of water that fills the tank so that less is used each time you flush.

WATER ACTION

- ○ If you have older, less efficient toilets, purchase a toilet dam for each toilet in your house. They should cost under $10 apiece and save 40% of the water per flush. Hardware stores may not routinely stock them, so you might have to ask your local hardware store to put in a special order.
- ○ Install the dam(s).
- ○ If you cannot get a commercial toilet dam, or don't wish to spend the money, make your own for free. While this homemade approach displaces only about 20% of the water per flush, it has an impact.

    Here's how to make a dam:
    - Clean an empty half-gallon plastic jug. Soak the jug to remove labels.
    - Fill the jug about half full with wet sand or gravel. Secure the lid tightly.
    - Put the jug in the corner of the tank, making sure it does not interfere with any moving parts.
    - Repeat these steps for each toilet in your home.

Note: You may want to go even further and consider replacing your toilet with a low-flow model. Some now require as little as 1.6 gallons per flush.

MATERIALS

Commercial toilet dam(s), or half-gallon jug(s) and lid(s), sand or gravel, or low-flow toilet(s)

TIME

Half an hour to purchase or assemble a dam or jug and a couple of minutes to install each one; longer to install a low-flow toilet

BENEFITS

A commercial dam will save you up to one gallon per flush or about 2,000 gallons a year. A homemade dam will save about half a gallon per flush, or about 1,000 gallons per year. These savings are just for one person. They will increase substantially based on the number of individuals in your household. For a small effort, you made a big contribution!

22. Am I Clean Yet?
Reducing Water Used for Showers and Baths

WHY ACT?

How much water do you need to get your body clean? The average shower uses five gallons per minute. This means you could save 25 gallons of water just by staying in the shower for five minutes instead of ten. By switching to a low-flow showerhead, you could save even more. A bath can use 30 to 60 gallons of water—over twice the amount you need for a five–minute shower. This water action will help you reduce your personal water use without sacrificing the pleasure of a warm shower. Now you have something to sing about as you lather up!

WATER ACTION

- ○ Time your average shower to become aware of your personal water use, and record the number of minutes it takes.
- ○ Determine how much time you actually need by taking your shower in a purposeful manner. Continue to time your shower for a few days until you get into the new habit.
- ○ A good goal to strive for is five minutes or under. To achieve this—or a time that better suits you—you can either take shorter showers or turn off the water while you are soaping up.
- ○ Catch warm-up water for your shower in a bucket or pan, and use to water plants or flush the toilet.

MATERIALS

A watch or clock, paper and pen

TIME

Here's one where you end up with more time

BENEFITS

You save five gallons for every minute less you shower or run the water, as well as energy to heat that water and electricity to pump it to you.

23. Go with the Flow
Reducing the Number of Toilet Flushes

WHY ACT?

Almost 30% of the water that comes into your home goes down the toilet. Every time you flush the average toilet, you use about 3.5 gallons of water. Even if you have a low-flow toilet, you still probably flush several times a day. Each flush uses fresh water, the same supply you need for other purposes, such as drinking, showering, laundering, and cleaning.

WATER ACTION

- ○ Here's the rule: "If it's yellow, let it mellow. If it's brown, flush it down."
- ○ Get members of your household together. Discuss this action and decide how many "pees in a pot" you want before flushing.

MATERIALS

None. But you may need to use some creative persuasion skills on your household and uninitiated friends

TIME

10 minutes to meet with household members

BENEFITS

If a household of 4 reduces its daily flushes from 20 to 10 or less, (at 3.5 gallons per flush) that would save about 35 gallons a day, or 12,500 gallons of water a year. That's enough to fill a small-sized swimming pool.

24. THE LAWN RANGER

Reducing Water Used for Lawns

WHY ACT?

If you have a lawn and water it, there's a good chance it's being overwatered by a third. The average quarter-acre of lawn gets about 22,000 gallons of water a week more than it needs! This water action will show you how the grass can be greener on your property. This is one of the most important water-saving efforts you can make.

WATER ACTION

❑ Most established lawns need only one inch of water a week. To give your lawn the inch it needs:

- Place three cans at various spots in one area of your lawn. Turn on the sprinkler and time how long it takes for one inch of water to accumulate in each can.
- Add the three times together, divide by three and that's how long you'll need to water that area.
- Each time you move your sprinkler, water for the same amount of time.

❑ To retain the water you use:

- Water early in the morning or early in the evening to avoid evaporation that occurs during the heat of the day.
- Keep your grass between 2" and 3" tall to provide natural shade that will help the soil stay moist. Leave grass clippings on the lawn to retain moisture (see *Cut It High and Let It Lie,* Action 4, pg. 11).

MATERIALS

Three cans, sprinkler, watch

TIME

A few minutes to calculate the amount of time you need to water; lots of time freed up by this new watering technique

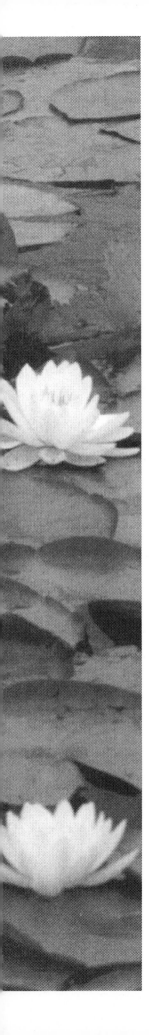

BENEFITS

You can save at least one-third of the water you now use by making sure your lawn only gets the inch of water it needs each week. Your water-saving habits are an important contribution to your community and planet.

25. A Master Waterer
Reducing Water Used for Gardening

WHY ACT?

If you have a garden, at least 50% of the water you use may be wasted through inefficiency. You probably use about 60 gallons of water every time you water for just 10 minutes. This water action will show you how to be a master waterer in your own little corner of paradise.

WATER ACTION

- ❍ Check all hose connections to make sure there are no leaks, and install hose washers where needed.
- ❍ Make sure your hose nozzle has an on-off switch (like a trigger mechanism).
- ❍ Water in the early morning or early evening to avoid evaporation that occurs during the heat of the day. Direct the water to the soil where it is needed. A deep soaking once a week is more effective than shallow watering every day.
- ❍ Cover your garden with a protective blanket of organic mulch, such as wood chips, to retain moisture.
- ❍ Whenever possible, landscape with native plants that require little water and upkeep.
- ❍ Use water collected in a rain barrel to water your landscaping (see *A No Rainer,* Action 10, pg. 20).

Note: To minimize your water use even more, you may want to consider using grey water (i.e., water saved from your sink, tub or shower to be re-used) or installing a drip irrigation system, which can save up to 50% of the water used with conventional methods.

MATERIALS

Hose washers, on-off switch, mulch, native plants

TIME

A few minutes to check for leaks and install washers; half an hour or more to add mulch, depending on the size of your garden; more time if you install a drip irrigation system; no extra time to set out native plants instead of others

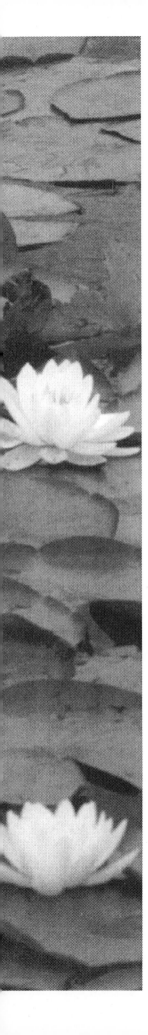

BENEFITS

By watering your garden more efficiently, you can save up to 50% of the water you normally use.

SECTION THREE:
HELPING OUT ACTIONS

HELPING OUT ACTION LOG

KEY:	
Average Time:	Typical Cost$
⧖ = 1 hour or less	♦ = low or no cost
⧖⧖ = 1–5 hours	♦♦ = $10–$100
⧖⧖⧖ = 5 hours or more	♦♦♦ = $100 plus

Action	Location	Time	Cost	Action Plan Date/Time	(✓) Discussed with Household
26. HOUSEHOLD BY HOUSEHOLD – Starting Neighborhood Water Stewardship Teams	Neighborhood	⧖	♦		
27. GO TEAM – Coaching Water Stewardship Teams	Neighborhood	⧖	♦		
28. APARTMENT/CONDOMINIUM DWELLERS TAKE CARE – Working with property managers and boards to adopt Water Stewardship practices	Yard	⧖⧖⧖	♦		
29. CITIZENHOOD – Contributing to your community's quality of life	Neighborhood	⧖	♦		
30. DUMP NO WASTE – Storm drain marking	Neighborhood	⧖	♦		
31. NEIGHBOR TO NATURE – Become a neighborhood stream steward	Neighborhood	⧖	♦		
32. NEIGHBORHOOD LIVABILITY – Starting a Livable Neighborhood team	Neighborhood	⧖	♦		

26. HOUSEHOLD BY HOUSEHOLD
Starting Neighborhood Water Stewardship Teams

WHY ACT?

Taking these actions helps our waterways become healthier. Helping others do the same is the next step. This water action will give you the chance to pass on what you have learned—person by person and household by household—until yours is a community of people committed to doing their part to ensure a better future for all of us.

WATER ACTION

○ Help create more Neighborhood Water Stewardship Teams. The goal is to have every team create at least one new team. Here's how:
- At the final meeting, speak with your team and determine if there is interest in starting more teams and specifically who would like to participate in this activity.
- If there is interest, organize an informational event for your block or immediate neighborhood.
- Set a date and follow the Team Initiator Guidelines, pg. 68 to form your team. The majority of people will be interested to attend an introductory event, if invited by their neighbors.

MATERIALS

A list of people to invite

TIME

A few minutes per person to invite them to your Neighborhood Water Stewardship Introduction event

BENEFITS

Each person you help to start on his or her journey can have similar positive environmental outcomes to yours. In this way, you can multiply your positive impact.

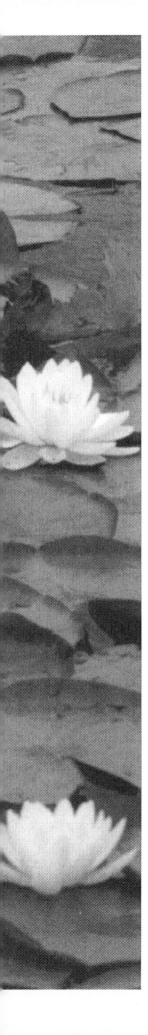

27. Go Team
Coaching Water Stewardship Teams

WHY ACT?

Becoming a water stewardship coach allows you to help others, your neighborhood, and the environment as a whole. For every team you start, at least five households begin stewarding our water resources. Coaching is also a way to keep yourself motivated to maintain the water practices you have begun. This water action makes you feel good while helping others do good.

WATER ACTION

- ○ At the final meeting of the program, let your team leader know that you are interested in being a team initiator.
- ○ Request support, if needed, to start your team.

MATERIALS

Section Five of this workbook

TIME

A couple of hours to review the support material, and several more hours to recruit team members and facilitate team meetings

BENEFITS

By empowering others to steward our water resources, you increase the positive impact you have in direct proportion to the number of people you coach!

28. APARTMENT/CONDOMINIUM DWELLERS TAKE CARE

Helping Property Managers and Boards Adopt Water-friendly Practices

WHY ACT?

Apartment and condominium residents can play an important role in increasing natural water filters and areas of wildlife habitat that benefit local streams. Because multi-family properties congregate many people together on a larger space than is typical of a single family dwelling, the rewards for planting this type of landscaping are great for local streams, wildlife, and residents. In addition, the apartment or condominium may save money as the use of water, pesticides, fertilizers, and maintenance and landscaping staff time decreases.

WATER ACTION

- ○ Read Actions 2, 3, 4, 10, 11, 12, 13, and 24 in this workbook to get ideas for the types of activities you can encourage at your apartment building or condominium. Make a list of the steps that will be required of property management and staff.
- ○ Do a survey to find out about current practices. Take a walk through the grounds to observe what is happening. If you live in an apartment, talk to the property manager or survey neighbors.
- ○ If you can, gather a team of concerned neighbors who would like to see some changes made. Management is more likely to listen to concerns voiced by a group, as opposed to one or two residents. One approach to demonstrate interest is to distribute a petition and ask your neighbors to sign it.
- ○ Make a presentation to your property manager or tenants' board about some of the changes they can make in their landscaping practices. Include information about why making these changes will benefit our streams and drinking water sources, as well as details about how the changes could save them money.
- ○ At the presentation, ask about when you should follow up and offer to gather any additional information to help them make a decision. Make sure you keep in touch as the issue progresses.
- ○ If the property manager or tenants' association makes changes to their landscaping practices, thank them. It is important for management to realize that residents pay attention to what they do.

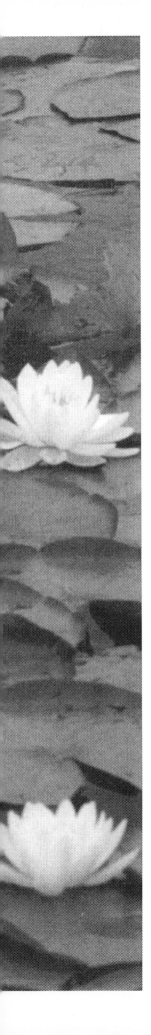

MATERIALS

Phone book, phone, computer for writing plans and petitions, and access to the Internet for research as needed

TIME

Up to 5 hours to research issues and voice information to the management; plus more hours depending on scope of changes and involvement from residents

BENEFITS

Depending on the actions implemented, you will prevent polluted stormwater from entering streams while making your property a natural place with attractive landscaping for you and your neighbors to enjoy.

29. CITIZENHOOD
Contributing to Your Community's Quality of Life

WHY ACT?

Getting involved in your local government's decision-making process is a very effective way to positively contribute to your neighborhood. During all the steps of the development process, your input can help determine zoning, the types of development, and details of the site plan. By advocating for low-impact design on new developments, you can have a major influence on your neighborhood's environmental impact and overall aesthetic.

WATER ACTION

- As a starting point, join your local civic or neighborhood association so you can learn about what is happening in your neighborhood and any local development projects that have the potential to impact local streams.
- If there is a specific development project of concern in process in your neighborhood, first find out all you can about what is happening. Contact your neighborhood civic association or the city or county planning commission.
- If there isn't one in place, form a neighborhood committee to develop a response to the proposed development. Put your ideas into writing. For site plans, aspects to consider include the footprint of the building, amount of parking and paved surfaces, and removal and planting of trees and shrubs. For areas where the land use has not yet been determined, ideas to suggest include a park, playground, or forested area, all of which will have significantly less impact on local waterways than a new building.
- Schedule a time to present your ideas to the entire neighborhood. If you live in an area represented by a civic association, ask to be added to the agenda of the next general meeting. Otherwise, schedule your own neighborhood meeting at the local school or community center.
- Depending on the timing of the project, other avenues to explore include participating in a planning commission meeting, writing a letter to the editor of the local paper, or speaking at a county board or city council meeting. Your local government may also have programs or grants available to make neighborhood improvements.
- If you are interested in more general participation, volunteer to serve on the planning commission, other local advisory group, or local land trust.

MATERIALS

Phone book, phone, computer for writing plans, and access to the Internet for research and contacting neighborhood associations and officials

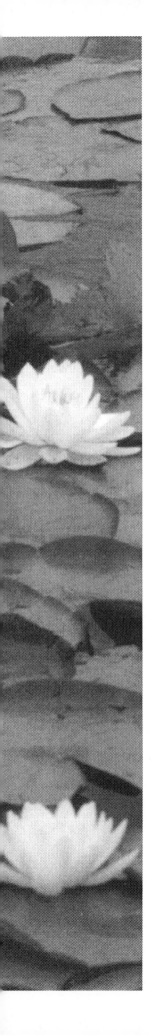

TIME

From two hours to attend a civic association meeting to several hours or more to organize a committee to respond to a local development project

BENEFITS

All local land use decisions directly affect the quality of water in our local streams. What you accomplish can range from saving trees on the site of a new development to creating a new neighborhood park to changing local policy.

30. DUMP NO WASTE
Storm Drain Marking and Maintenance

WHY ACT?

Only a small percentage of the country's storm drains connect to sewage treatment facilities. For the most part, storm drains mainline their contents straight to a water body. The health of all life on Earth is linked to the health of our waterways. We all know that the nation's water has become increasingly unsafe to drink, but here's the zinger: according to EPA, over 60% of the pollution comes from urban and agricultural stormwater runoff, not industry. Used motor oil, antifreeze, household chemicals, pesticides, and chemical fertilizers get much of the blame. Intentionally pouring these materials in storm drains in the mistaken belief that they get filtered at the sewage treatment plant does much damage.

Most localities have a storm drain marking program that engages volunteers in gluing vinyl markers to storm drains to remind people not to dump. Studies show that over 75% of people who see marked storm drains knew where their water went, compared to about a third of those who do not see a marked drain. People are more likely to change their behavior to prevent pollution once they understand the storm water runoff destination. This water action will show you how to play an important role in your neighborhood for the good of your environment.

WATER ACTION

- ○ Use your team to do storm drain marking in your neighborhood. Check with your local government stormwater management agency to get supplies. Schedule a date and make sure to coordinate any permits needed from the local utility and Public Works Department. On the day of the storm drain marking, some team members can glue the markers on the storm drains and others can educate the neighborhood by passing out door-hangers that tell the storm drain/watershed story.
- ○ Your team can also "adopt" neighborhood drains to keep them swept free of debris. This requires sweeping the area near the storm drain regularly to keep it free of leaf litter and debris.
- ○ "Adopt your watershed" by having team members do a study and educate the rest of the team. The easiest way to do this is to go to EPA's excellent web site: www.epa.gov/surf. There you'll learn everything you need to know about how your storm drain fits into one of the country's 21 watershed regions, 222 subregions, 352 accounting units, and 2,262 cataloguing units. A real eye-opener.

MATERIALS

Storm drain markers, door hangers, glue, wire brush, gloves, brooms, trash bags

TIME

An hour to call and recruit volunteers for your storm drain-marking teams; an hour or so to mark drains; a few hours to "adopt" your watershed, and more if you decide to "adopt" a storm drain

BENEFITS

Cleaner drops in the bucket of the planet's water.

31. NEIGHBOR TO NATURE
Become a Neighborhood Water Steward

WHY ACT?

Our actions can make a big difference in the overall health of wildlife and the quality of our water. Cleaning up stream and river banks not only makes our natural areas look much better, but it prevents trash from being swept downstream and harming aquatic life. Riparian zone (i.e., streambank) restoration helps prevent erosion, keeping our waterways clearer and free of sediment that can smother plants and animals.

Another reason to take care of our local watershed is that besides being a natural treasure, it is also a great economic resource. It is up to all of us to do our part to reduce the pollution we send downstream.

WATER ACTION

- ○ Bring your team to a stream/river cleanup or storm drain marking event! Your team can also organize its own service project.
- ○ Volunteer to help your local government in stream monitoring efforts.
- ○ Work with your city/county to Adopt-a-Stream, and help to maintain part of a stream or river near you.
- ○ Become a Water Steward. Lead community volunteer events and deliver classroom presentations on watershed protection.
- ○ Involve your team in a stream restoration project. Contact your local government for information on upcoming events.

MATERIALS

Shoes for getting wet—either waterproof boots or old sneakers, rubber gloves (e.g. dishwashing gloves), long sleeves and pants for protection against poison ivy, and 1 to 3 trash bags per person for stream cleanups

TIME

In just a couple of hours, your team can have a huge impact on a section of a stream or river

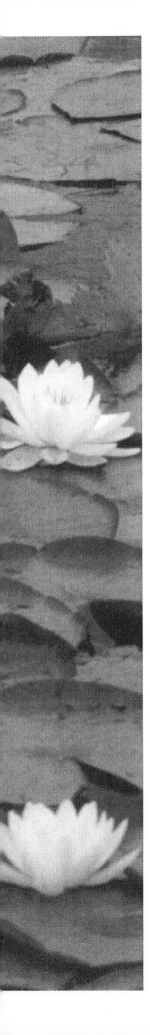

BENEFITS

Helping to clean up your community's streams and rivers will make it more attractive and reduce impact on local wildlife and waterways.

32. NEIGHBORHOOD LIVABILITY
Starting a Livable Neighborhood Team

WHY ACT?

Households that completed the Water Stewardship Program asked how they could use what they had learned to improve the overall livability of their neighborhood. This question spawned an obvious idea—extend the program beyond water to the entire neighborhood. The Livable Neighborhood Program helps neighbors create and act on their own visions of how they can transform their neighborhood into the kind of place they'd like it to be. This action helps you and your team take the work you have begun to the next level.

WATER ACTION

- ○ Go to the Empowerment Institute web site, www.empowermentinstitute.net and click on Livable Neighborhood Program. Review the information and print it out for your team.
- ○ Present this idea to your team and encourage them to do the program.
- ○ If they accept, order workbooks and start the program.

MATERIALS

The Livable Neighborhood Program workbook can be ordered from the web site

TIME

A few minutes to view our web site, 10-15 minutes to enroll your team

BENEFITS

A cleaner, safer, healthier, friendlier neighborhood that is kinder to the environment.

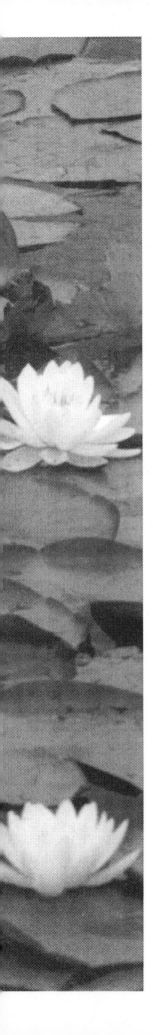

NOTES

_____

_____

_____

_____

_____

_____

_____

_____

_____

Section Four:
Water Stewardship Assessment

Use this Water Assessment to help determine the actions you will take to reduce your impact on water quality and water use.

Before you start the program, check which actions you have already fully done and the ones you will do. After you complete an action, put a check in the Done box.

At the end of the program, team members report the number of actions in their Done column.

SECTION ONE: WATER QUALITY ACTIONS

Actions	Did fully before	Will do	Done	N/A
1. Toxic Sleuth – Reducing toxic products in your home I use non-toxic cleaning products in my home.	☐	☐	☐	☐
2. A Natural Lawn – Reducing the use of weed killers and fertilizers on your lawn I use an organic or slow-release fertilizer on my lawn. I hand pull weeds to avoid using chemicals. I overseed my lawn to crowd out weeds.	☐ ☐ ☐	☐ ☐ ☐	☐ ☐ ☐	☐ ☐ ☐
3. A Green Gardener – Reducing the use of toxic pesticides, herbicides, and fertilizers in your garden My garden has pest- and drought-resistant native plants. I manage garden pests without using toxic pesticides.	☐ ☐	☐ ☐	☐ ☐	☐ ☐
4. Cut It High and Let It Lie – Mulching grass When my lawn is mowed, the grass clipping are left to mulch.	☐	☐	☐	☐
5. Let It Rot – Backyard composting I compost my food wastes. I compost my yard wastes.	☐ ☐	☐ ☐	☐ ☐	☐ ☐
6. Poop Scoop – Cleaning up after your dog I clean up my dog's poop and dispose of it properly.	☐	☐	☐	☐
7. Don't Be an Oil Drip – Identifying and fixing oil leaks on your vehicle(s) The oil leaks I identified have been fixed.	☐	☐	☐	☐

Continued on next page

Actions	Did fully before	Will do	Done	N.
8. No Phos-for-Us – Washing your car with the least environmental impact I use biodegradable phosphate-free soap to wash my car. I avoid having my car waste water go into the sewer. I use a hose with an on/off nozzle to wash my car.	☐ ☐ ☐	☐ ☐ ☐	☐ ☐ ☐	☐ ☐ ☐
9. Down by the Stream – Creating a streamside "Grow Zone" I live near a stream that has many native plants on its banks. I am restoring an eroding streamside.	☐ ☐	☐ ☐	☐ ☐	☐ ☐
10. A No Rainer – Installing a rain barrel or cistern. The gutters on my house are free of debris. The gutters on my house direct rainwater into my yard or rain barrel.	☐ ☐	☐ ☐	☐ ☐	☐ ☐
11. Catch It While You Can – Creating a rain garden I have created a rain garden in my yard.	☐	☐	☐	☐
12. Yard Makeover – Creating Water-friendly landscaping I have aerated and amended my soil to absorb more rainwater. I have a rain garden to absorb water in my yard depressions.	☐ ☐	☐ ☐	☐ ☐	☐ ☐
13. Let the Ground Show Through – Reducing paved surfaces I have a plan to reduce or limit the paved surfaces around my home.	☐	☐	☐	☐
14. The Road Less Traveled – Reducing Vehicle Miles Traveled I have reduced the number of miles I drive each week. I carpool whenever possible. I use public transportation.	☐ ☐ ☐	☐ ☐ ☐	☐ ☐ ☐	☐ ☐ ☐
15. Leak Not – Finding and fixing leaks in your fuel storage tank I have performed a home audit on my fuel storage tank(s). I have repaired or replaced leaking fuel storage tank(s).	☐ ☐	☐ ☐	☐ ☐	☐ ☐

Section Two: Water Conservation Actions

Actions	Did fully before	Will do	Done	N/A
16. Aqua Cop – Finding and fixing water leaks in your home I have checked for water leaks in my home. I have fixed the water leaks in my home.	☐ ☐	☐ ☐	☐ ☐	☐ ☐
17. Aqua Tech – Installing water-saving devices I have low-flow shower head(s) in my home. I have water aerator(s) on my faucets.	☐ ☐	☐ ☐	☐ ☐	☐ ☐
18. Scrub-a-Dub-Rub – Reducing water used for personal care I turn off the water while shaving, brushing my teeth, and washing my hands or face.	☐	☐		☐
19. Scrub-a-Dub Tub – Reducing water used to wash dishes I have reduced the number of times per week I use my dishwasher. I only run my dishwasher when it's full. When I wash dishes by hand I don't leave the water running.	☐ ☐ ☐	☐ ☐ ☐	☐ ☐ ☐	☐ ☐ ☐
20. All Bottled Up – Drinking refrigerated water My household members drink tap water from a refrigerated container instead of running the tap until the water gets cold.	☐	☐	☐	☐
21. Tanks a Lot – Reducing water used for toilet flushing The toilets in my house are low-flow. The toilets in my house have a toilet dam. The toilets in my house have plastic jugs.	☐ ☐ ☐	☐ ☐ ☐	☐ ☐ ☐	☐ ☐ ☐
22. Am I Clean Yet? – Reducing water used for showers and baths I have reduced my shower time to 5 minutes or less. Other household members have reduced their shower time to 5 minutes or less.	☐ ☐	☐ ☐	☐ ☐	☐ ☐
23. Go with the Flow – Reducing the number of toilet flushes I have reduced the times a day a toilet is flushed in my home.	☐	☐	☐	☐
24. The Lawn Ranger – Reducing water used for your lawn I have reduced the amount of water I use for my lawn. I water my lawn early in the day or after dusk. I grow my grass 2 to 3 inches before I mow.	☐ ☐ ☐	☐ ☐ ☐	☐ ☐ ☐	☐ ☐ ☐
25. Master Waterer – Reducing water used for gardening My hose or sprinkler do not have leaks. I water my garden early in the day or after dark. I use mulch in my garden to help retain moisture. I use drip irrigation. I use grey water. My yard has native or drought tolerant plants that survive on native rainfall.	☐ ☐ ☐ ☐ ☐ ☐	☐ ☐ ☐ ☐ ☐ ☐	☐ ☐ ☐ ☐ ☐ ☐	☐ ☐ ☐ ☐ ☐ ☐
Tally up the total of actions taken.				

Section Five:

Program Support Tools

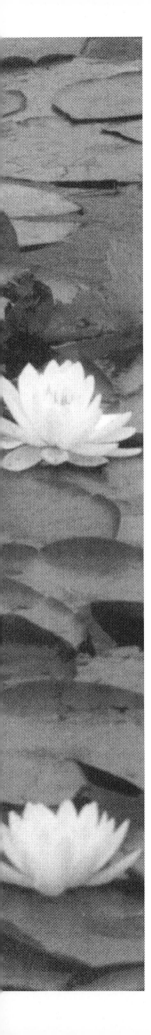

INTRODUCTION

This section provides a support structure to help you effectively implement the program. It includes:

Team Initiator Guidelines: A 5-step process for starting your team.

Information Meeting Guide: A script for conducting an informational meeting for potential team members. It is also possible to use elements for one-on-one communications.

Team-Building Meeting Guide: A script for conducting the first team meeting. This team can consist of household members or 5 to 8 friends, neighbors, colleagues, or faith community members. The focus of the meeting is to create a support system, learn how to to assess your water use, and develop your action plan to reduce your negative impact.

Topic Meeting Guides: These scripts are for meetings 2 to 4. The goal in these meetings is for team participants to report on actions taken, describe action plans for the next section, and get support.

TEAM INITIATOR GUIDELINES

1. If you are starting the team, you are the team initiator. To learn about the program, read the introduction, how the program works, the table of contents, and review the actions.

2. Set a date and time for hosting a Team Building Meeting either in your home or at some other location.

3. Create your team. This can consist of family, friends, neighbors, co-workers, or members of your faith community or civic organization. Choose the community that is easiest to pull together. The best size for a team is 5–8 households. If that is not possible, your household unit can become the team. If potential team members wish to know more about the program, invite them to visit www.empowermentinstitute.net/files/WSP.html.

4.. Each household will need to have a copy of this book. It can be purchased online at www.empowermentinstitute.net, or mail a check for $12.95 plus $3.95 for shipping and handling per book to Empowerment Institute, PO Box 428, Woodstock, NY, 12498.

5. You are responsible for leading the 4 meetings. Meeting scripts are located in this section. Before the Team Building Meeting, review the guide, fill in your water assessment, and choose the actions you will do.

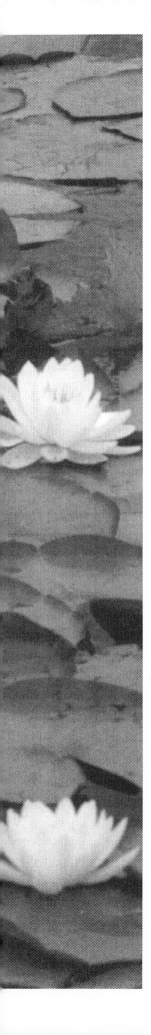

INFORMATION MEETING GUIDE

BEFORE EVENT

○ If possible, serve light refreshments and set up room in a U shape to increase sense of intimacy.

○ Review this guide before the meeting so that you are familiar with the process.

AGENDA (Times Approximate)

1. Welcome, Purpose, Agenda - 10 minutes
2. Introductions - 15 minutes
3. Overview of Challenge - 15 minutes
4. Program Description - 10 minutes
5. Q & A - 15 minutes
6. Invitation to Participate on a Team - 10 minutes
7. Team Program Sign-up and Placement - 15 minutes
Total Time: 90 minutes

1. Welcome, Purpose, Agenda - 10 minutes

○ Welcome: Welcome and appreciate people for coming. State your name and role as the team initiator.

○ Purpose: To become a better steward of our community's and planet's precious water resources. Add your personal motivation for organizing this event.

○ Agenda: Introductions, overview of challenge, program description, Q & A, invitation to participate.

2. Introductions - 15 minutes

○ Invite participants to state name, where they live, and any other important information and to say what they would like out of the meeting. If a large group, limit the sharing to 8-10 people.

3. Overview of Challenge - 15 minutes

○ This program will help us learn practices to develop a water-friendly lifestyle, and improve the environmental quality of our neighborhood and community.

○ Read out key passages from the Introduction.

○ This gathering will give you a taste of the program so you can decide if this is something you would like to do. And for those who are motivated to get this going in your neighborhood, we'll get started tonight at the end of the meeting.

4. Program Description - 10 minutes

○ Show copy of this book and read "How the Program Works"

5. Q & A - 15 minutes

○ Invite questions about the program and their participation. Draw out any concerns that individuals might have about participation.

6. Invitation to Participate on a Team - 10 minutes

○ Ask how many are interested in participating in the program? Acknowledge those that raise their hand and draw out any concerns from those who didn't. For those who can't join now, invite them to do the program on their own or join a team in the future.

○ Invite participants to spread the word to others and have them contact you if they wish to participate on a team. Provide your name, e-mail, and phone number on a flip chart if available.

7. Team Program Sign Up and Placement - 15 minutes

○ If several teams are formed, organize in groups of 5-8 households by proximity, affinity, or other criteria.

○ All can meet at one location and then divide up into sub-groups of 5-8 households or can divide up into separate teams. In either case, request a volunteer from each team to serve as team leader. Point them to the meeting guides that tell them how to lead the meetings.

○ Set date(s) for the Team Building Meeting.

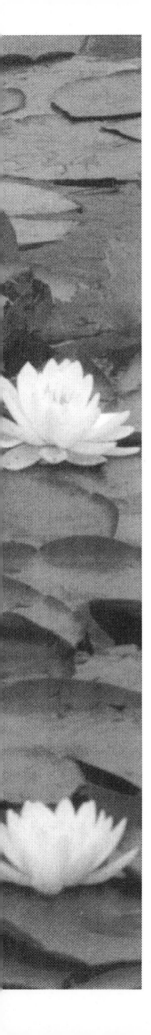

TEAM BUILDING MEETING GUIDE

BEFORE EVENT

○ Review this meeting guide.

○ Fill in the Water Stewardship Assessment *Did Fully Before* and *Will Do* boxes on pages 65-67.

○ Fill in the Action Log for Sections One (page 5) and Section Two (page 35) with the *Will Do* actions from the assessment.

○ Be prepared to answer questions your team might have about the process

AGENDA (Times Approximate)

1. Welcome, Purpose, Overview - 15 minutes
2. Participants State Reasons for Joining - 20 minutes
3. Review How Program Works - 10 minutes
4. Review the Water Assessment - 10 minutes
5. Review Workbook and Action Log - 20 minutes
6. Schedule Meetings - 15 minutes
7. Next Steps - 5 minutes
Total Time - 1.5 to 2 Hours

1. Welcome, Purpose, Overview – 15 minutes

○ Welcome participants and thank them for coming. State why you were motivated to form this team.

○ Indicate that the purpose of this meeting is to be a better steward of our precious water resources.

○ Read aloud the introduction to the book on page 1.

2. Participants State Reasons for Participating – 20 minutes

○ Ask team members to state their name, where they live (if relevant), and why they chose to participate.

○ Write down why each person chose to participate.

○ At the end, summarize the key reasons individuals chose to participate. Create into a team statement of purpose. Invite team members to write this in their book.

3. Review How Program Works – 10 minutes

○ Review the seven points from pages 2 and 3.

4. Review Water Assessment – 10 minutes

○ Share your assessment results and what you learned.

○ Have team members fill in the *Did Fully Before* box and the *Will Do* box.

5. Review Workbook and Action Log – 20 minutes

○ Invite an individual to read aloud the actions in the table of contents to familiarize the team with the program content.

○ Have team members transfer their *Will Do* actions from the Water Assessment to the Action Logs located at the beginning of sections one and two.

○ Review the format of one action from each of the three sections.

○ Answer any questions about this process.

6. Schedule Meetings – 15 minutes

○ Schedule the next 3 meetings, allowing 10-14 days between meetings to take the actions.

○ Request that everyone commit to coming on time and you will commit to ending within 2 hours of the start time.

○ If something unexpected occurs and someone cannot attend a meeting, request that the person notify you in advance and provide you with their action log. You will call them after the meeting to let them know what happened.

7. Review Next Steps – 5 minutes

○ Complete your Water Stewardship Lifestyle Assessment.

○ Read the workbook Introduction and Water Quality section.

○ Fill in your Water Quality Action Log

○ Come to the meeting with any actions for which you might need support from a teammate.

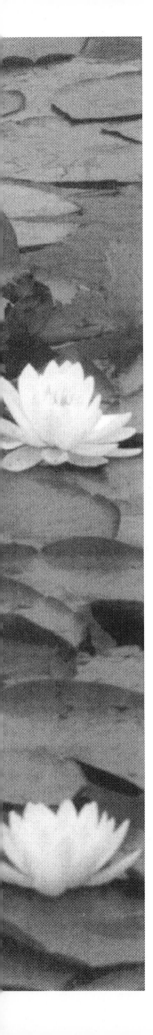

TOPIC MEETING ONE GUIDE: WATER QUALITY

BEFORE MEETING

- ○ Read this meeting guide carefully and plan in advance what you will do for agenda items 1, 3, and 4.
- ○ Complete your Water Quality Action Log in the workbook.
- ○ Do any of the Water Quality actions you wish to demonstrate
- ○ Call team members to confirm time and date of the next meeting.

BRING TO THE MEETING

- ○ Examples of the materials you are using to take the Water Quality actions, such as non-toxic home and yard products, poop scoop, yard composter, etc.
- ○ This book.

AGENDA (Times Approximate)

1. Inspirational Start - 5 minutes
2. Review the Water Stewardship Lifestyle Assessments - 20 minutes
3. Do a Water Quality demonstration - 5 minutes
4. Review Water Quality actions - 15 minutes
5. Team members share Action Logs and get support - 20 minutes
6. Schedule times for support calls - 5 minutes
7. Explore how the team is doing - 10 minutes
8. Review what the team needs to do before next meeting - 5 minutes
9. Celebrate the team's accomplishments - 5 minutes
Total Time: 1 hour 30 minutes

1. Inspirational Start – 5 minutes

- ○ Start with a brief poem, quote, personal anecdote, or something that connects the group to the meaning and larger purpose of what you are doing.

2. Review the Water Stewardship Lifestyle Assessment – 20 minutes

- ○ Have each household share their assessment and the actions they will do. Invite reflection from individuals from doing this exercise.

3. Demonstrate Action(s) – 5 minutes

○ Demonstrate one or more actions you think might be helpful to the team. Show what you did and how you did it so the team can learn from your hands-on experience.

4. Review Water Quality Actions – 15 minutes

○ Go through the actions of the Water Quality section of the workbook.

○ Highlight each action.

5. Team Members Share Action Logs and Get Support – 20 minutes

○ Review your Action Log with the team to demonstrate how to use the Action Log format in the workbook. Be sure to give the date and time you plan to do the actions. This will model the process of thoughtful time management and your commitment.

○ Have each member share their Action Log with the team.

○ Have team talk about and choose any Water Quality actions they can do together.

○ Have team members ask for support (if needed) to complete the actions they have chosen.

6. Check-In on Team Performance – 10 minutes

○ At each meeting take a little time to look at how the team is functioning and tune up as needed. A team that is committed to mutual accountability achieves the best results from this peer-support system.

○ If any team members came late, request that they come on time in the future so the meeting can be run without interruptions. If a number of people came late, requiring you to delay the start of the meeting, request that they come on time so you can end on time. If people can't get there at the agreed upon time, ask if people would like to start the meeting later.

○ If anyone did not attend, call and ask the person if he/she is still committed to participating in the program. If so, request the person prioritize attending the following meetings. Explain what happened at this meeting.

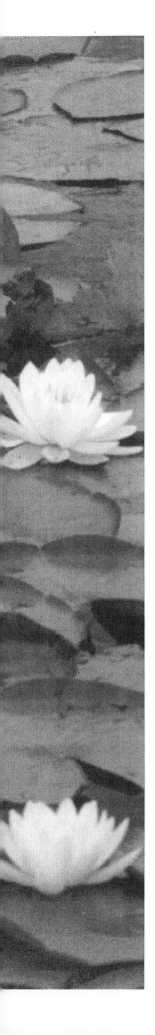

7. Set Up Support Calls – 5 minutes

○ *Approximately half way between this meeting and the next, you as team leader are encouraged to call team members to see how they are doing in implementing their action plans. Left on our own, our motivation often wanes. These support calls make a big difference in assisting team members to stay on track.*

○ Arrange mutually convenient times for checking in with team members. Allow up to 10 minutes per call. If person is not there for the agreed upon call, leave a message and request a call back.

8. Review Next Steps – 5 minutes

○ Take the Water Quality actions you've planned.

○ Read the Water Conservation actions in the workbook and fill in your Water Conservation Action Log.

○ Get support from the team to complete all the selected actions.

9. Acknowledge Team's Accomplishments – 10 minutes

○ Express your appreciation to team members for what they have accomplished. State in a sentence or two what was most meaningful for you and invite others to do the same. If appropriate, end with some type of celebration.

Topic Meeting Two Guide: Water Conservation

BEFORE MEETING

○ Read the Water Conservation section of the workbook.

○ Complete your Water Conservation Action Log.

○ Do any of the Water Conservation actions you wish to demonstrate in your own home before the team meeting.

○ Call team members to confirm time and date of the next meeting.

BRING TO THE MEETING

○ Examples of the materials you are using to take the water actions, such as low flow showerheads or faucet aerator.

○ This book.

AGENDA (Times Approximate)

1. Inspirational Start - 5 minutes
2. Fill in *Done* column of Water Quality Assessment - 5 minutes
3. Share experiences with Water Quality actions - 15 minutes
4. Do Water Conservation demonstration - 5 minutes
5. Review Water Conservation actions - 15 minutes
6. Team members share Action Logs and get support - 20 minutes
7. Schedule times for support calls - 5 minutes
8. Explore how the team is doing - 10 minutes
9. Review what the team needs to do before next meeting - 5 minutes
10. Celebrate the team's accomplishments - 5 minutes
Total Time: 1 hour 30 minutes

1. Inspirational Start – 5 minutes

○ Start with a brief poem, personal anecdote, song, prayer or something inspirational that connects the group to the meaning and larger purpose of what you are doing

2. Fill in *Done* Column of Water Quality Assessment – 5 minutes

○ Fill in the *Done* column of the assessment for the Water Quality actions you have completed.

○ Put in a pledge date for actions that are seasonal.

3. Share Experiences with Water Quality Actions – 15 minutes

○ Have people share the actions they took, what they learned, and where, if anywhere, they encountered a problem and how they addressed it.

○ Acknowledge team members for what has been accomplished.

4. Do Water Conservation Action Demonstration – 5 minutes

○ Demonstrate one or more actions you think might be helpful to the team. Show what you did and how you did it so the team can learn from your hands-on experience.

5. Review Water Conservation Actions – 30 minutes

○ Go through the actions of the Water Conservation section of the workbook

○ Highlight each action.

6. Team Members Share Action Logs and Get Support – 20 minutes

○ Review your Action Log with the team to demonstrate how to use the Action Log format in the workbook. Be sure to give the date and time you plan to do the actions. This will model the process of thoughtful time management and your commitment.

○ Have each member share their Action Log with the team.

○ Have team talk about and choose any Water Conservation actions they can do together.

○ Have team members ask for support (if needed) to complete the actions they have chosen.

7. Check-In on Team Performance – 10 minutes

○ At each meeting take a little time to look at how the team is functioning and tune up as needed. A team that is committed to mutual accountability achieves the best results from this peer-support system.

○ If any team members came late, request that they come on time in the future so the meeting can be run without interruptions. If a number of people came late, requiring you to delay the start of the meeting, request that they come on time so you can end on time. If people can't get there at the agreed upon time, ask if people would like to start the meeting later.

○ If anyone did not attend, call and ask the person if he/she is still committed to participating in the program. If so, request the person prioritize attending the remaining meetings. Explain what happened at the meeting they missed.

8. Set Up Support Calls – 5 minutes

○ *Approximately half way between this meeting and the next, you as team leader are encouraged to call team members to see how they are doing in implementing their actions. Left on our own, our motivation often wanes. These support calls make a big difference in assisting team members to stay on track.*

○ Arrange mutually convenient times for checking in with team members. Allow up to 10 minutes per call. If the person is not there for the agreed upon call, leave a message and request a call back.

9. Review Next Steps – 5 minutes

○ Take the Water Conservation actions you've planned.

○ Read the Helping Out actions in the workbook and fill in your Helping Out Action Log.

○ Get support as needed from the team to complete all selected actions.

10. Acknowledge Team's Accomplishments – 10 minutes

○ Express your appreciation to team members for what they have accomplished. State in a sentence or two what was most meaningful for you and invite others to do the same. If appropriate, end with some type of celebration.

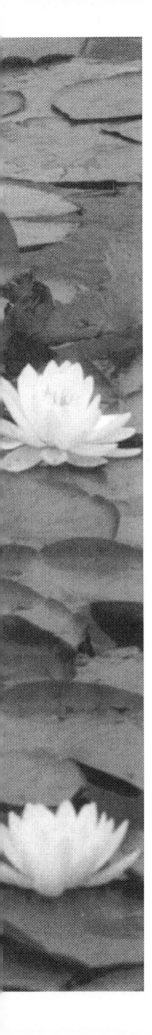

TOPIC MEETING THREE GUIDE: HELPING OUT

BEFORE MEETING

○ Read the Helping Out section of the workbook

○ Call team members to confirm time and date of the meeting.

○ Remind team members to bring their Water Stewardship Assessment to be completed and shared at the end of the meeting.

BRING TO THE MEETING

○ This book.

AGENDA (Times Approximate)

1. Inspirational Start - 5 minutes
2. Fill in *Done* column of Water Conservation Assessment - 5 minutes
3. Share experiences with Water Conservation actions - 15 minutes
4. Review Helping Out actions - 20 minutes
5. Team members share Action Logs and get support - 20 minutes
6. Schedule times for support calls - 5 minutes
7. Explore how the team is doing - 10 minutes
8. Review what the team needs to do before next meeting - 5 minutes
9. Celebrate the team's accomplishments - 5 minutes
Total Time: 1 hour 30 minutes

1. Inspirational Start and Check-in – 5 minutes

○ Welcome everyone. Start with a brief poem, personal anecdote, song, prayer, or something inspirational that connects the group to the meaning and larger purpose of what you are doing.

2. Fill in *Done* Column of Water Conservation Assessment – 5 minutes

○ Fill in the *Done* column of the assessment for the Water Conservation actions you have completed.

○ Ask if people have put in a pledge date for actions that are seasonal.

3. Share Experiences with Water Conservation Actions – 15 minutes

○ Have people share the actions they took, what they learned and where, if anywhere, they encountered a problem and how they addressed it.

○ Acknowledge team members for what has been accomplished.

4. Review Helping Out Actions – 15 minutes

○ Go through the actions of the Helping Out section of the workbook.

○ Highlight each action.

5. Team Members Share Action Logs and Get Support – 20 minutes

○ Review your Helping Out Action Log with the team to demonstrate how to use the Action Log format in the workbook. Be sure to give the date and time you plan to do the actions. This will model the process of thoughtful time management and your commitment.

○ Have each member share their Helping Out Action Log with the team.

○ Have team talk about and choose any Helping Out actions they can do together.

6. Check-In on Team Performance – 10 minutes

○ At each meeting take a little time to look at how the team is functioning and tune up as needed. A team that is committed to mutual accountability achieves the best results from this peer-support system.

○ If any team members came late, request that they come on time in the future so the meeting can be run without interruptions. If a number of people came late, requiring you to delay the start of the meeting, request that they come on time so you can end on time. If people can't get there at the agreed upon time, ask if people would like to start the meeting later.

○ If anyone did not attend, call and ask the person if he/she is still committed to participating in the program. If so, request that the person prioritize attending the remaining meetings. Explain what happened at the meeting they missed.

7. Set Up Support Calls – 5 minutes

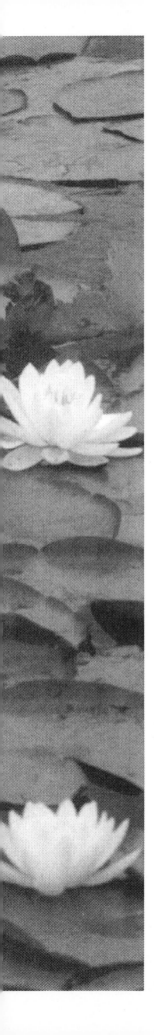

○ *Approximately half way between this meeting and the next, you as team leader are encouraged to call team members to see how they are doing in implementing their actions. Left on our own, our motivation often wanes. These support calls make a big difference in assisting team members to stay on track.*

○ Arrange mutually convenient times for checking in with team members. Allow up to 10 minutes per call. If the person is not there for the agreed upon call, leave a message and request a call back.

9. Review Next Steps – 5 minutes

○ Take the Helping Out actions you've planned.

○ Complete anything from the past not yet finished

○ Get support if needed from the team to complete all selected actions.

○ Plan next meeting if you want to continue as a team.

9. Acknowledge Team's Accomplishments – 10 minutes

○ Express your appreciation to team members for what they have accomplished. State in a sentence or two what was most meaningful for you and invite others to do the same. If appropriate, end with some type of celebration.

ABOUT THE AUTHOR

David Gershon, founder and CEO of Empowerment Institute, is one of the world's leading authorities on behavior change and large-scale transformation. He applies his expertise to various issues requiring community, organizational, or societal transformation. His clients range from large cities and organizations to social entrepreneurs and transformational small businesses. He has addressed issues ranging from environmental behavior change to emergency preparedness; from organizational talent development to low-income neighborhood revitalization. Longitudinal research studies indicate that adopted behavior changes are sustained over time.

He conceived and organized, in partnership with the United Nations Children's Fund and ABC Television, one of the planet's first major global initiatives, the First Earth Run. At the height of the Cold War, using the mythic power of relaying fire around the world, millions of people, in partnership with the world's political leaders and media, participated in creating a profound sense of our connectedness.

David is the author of nine books including the bestselling *Empowerment: The Art of Creating Your Life As You Want It*, which has become a classic on the subject. He has also written the popular *Low Carbon Diet: A 30 Day Program to Lose 5,000 Pounds*. He is currently writing *Reinventing the Social Change Formula: A New Approach to Changing Behavior in Society*. Considered a master personal development trainer, he co-directs the Empowerment Institute Certification Program, a school for transformative change. He has lectured at Harvard, MIT, and Duke and served as an advisor to the Clinton White House and United Nations on behavior change and sustainability issues. His work has received considerable media attention and many honors.

For more information visit www.empowermentinstitute.net. David can be contacted at dgershon@empowermentinstitute.net.

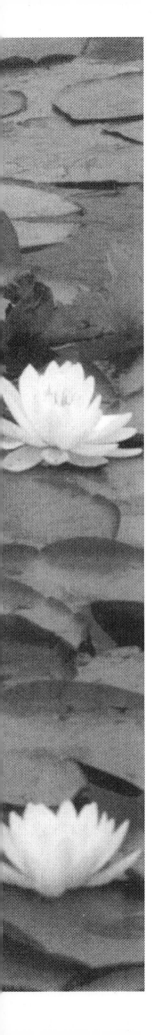

OTHER PROGRAMS AND BOOKS BY DAVID GERSHON

Water Stewardship—This book can be used as part of a residential non point source behavior change and outreach capacity building program to address residential non point source pollution and water conservation. For more information visit www.empowermentinstitute.net.

Empowerment Institute Certification Program—Over the past 25 years, Empowerment Institute has developed a highly effective transformational social change leadership program. It certifies *Water Stewardship* Program leaders in using these transformational and community empowerment tools. To learn more visit www.empowermentinstitute.net.

Changing the World: The Craft of Transformative Leadership—This two-day training provides skills and inspiration for leaders implementing transformative change in an organization or community. It is customized for organizations or communities. For more information visit www.empowermentinstitute.net.

Low Carbon Diet: A 30 Day Program to Lose 5000 Pounds—Grounded in over two decades of environmental behavior change research, this illustrated workbook offers readers much more than a to-do list of eco-friendly actions. With practicality and humor, bestselling author and environmental change pioneer David Gershon walks readers through every step of the carbon-reduction process, from calculating their current CO_2 footprint to tracking their progress and measuring their impact. By making simple changes to actions they take every day, readers learn how to reduce their annual household CO_2 output by at least 15%. And, for those who are more ambitious, there are chapters on how to help one's workplace, local schools, and community do the same. For more information visit www.empowermentinstitute.net/lcd.

Cool Community Campaign—The Cool Community Campaign engages local organizations across all sectors (including government, environmental organizations, businesses, neighborhood associations, faith-based groups, service clubs, and educational institutions) in a two-year campaign to engage up to 85% of the citizenry in *Low Carbon Diet's* proven program for household CO_2-reduction. The goal of the initiative is to help community residents reduce their carbon-footprint 20% by 2010. The first communities to achieve this goal will also serve as prototypes for the many cities and towns throughout America and around the world who are seeking effective climate change solutions. For more information visit www.empowermentinstitute.net/lcd.

Livable Neighborhood Program: Making Life Better on the Street Where You Live—This program has been successfully used in many communities to help neighbors improve the quality of life on their block. The action format is similar to *Water Stewardship* but it is done as a team rather than an individual household. The program is divided into four sections: neighborhood health and safety, neighborhood beautification and greening, neighborhood resource sharing, and neighborhood community building. For more information visit www.empowermentinstitute.net.

All Together Now: Neighbors Helping Neighbors Create a Disaster Resilient Community—This program helps residents prepare for natural disasters, terrorist incidents, emergencies, or an avian flu pandemic. It uses the same action format as *Water Stewardship* and is done either as a team or single household. It is designed to create disaster resilient blocks and buildings. For more information visit www.empowermentinstitute.net.

EcoTeam: Empowering Americans to Create Earth Friendly Lifestyles—This is the mother program that has been adapted for 22 countries. It is designed to help participants create environmentally sustainable lifestyles. It focuses on garbage, water, energy, transportation, and purchasing. It can be done as a single household or EcoTeam. For more information visit www.empowermentinstitute.net.

Journey for the Planet: A Kid's Five Week Adventure to Create an Earth Friendly Life—This is the children's version of the EcoTeam program. It can be done by children on their own or as part of a classroom or youth group. A teacher's curriculum is available for use in the classroom. This program is described in the "Cool School" action of the *Low Carbon Diet*. For more information visit www.empowermentinstitute.net/journey.

Dream for Our World—This book tells the mythic story of the First Earth Run and provides 7 practices that grew out of it for changing the world. For more information visit www.empowermentinstitute.net.

Empowerment: The Art of Creating Your Life As You Want It—Now in its 11th printing, and translated into eight languages, *Empowerment: The Art of Creating Your Life As You Want It* is widely considered to be a classic in the field of personal empowerment and transformation. Based on David Gershon and Gail Straub's two decades of work helping thousands of people create the life of their dreams, the book guides readers step-by-step through a systematic self-transformation program addressing seven key areas of life: relationships, sexuality, money, work, body, emotions, and spirituality. Its simple premise— that our thoughts and beliefs create the conditions of our life—is illustrated with anecdotes from each of the seven areas. Readers are then given practical and immediately applicable tools to help envision and create what they wish to achieve in each of these areas.